Animas Quilts

Durango, Colorado USA

Jackie Robinson

Acknowledgments

My greatest appreciation goes to the eight ladies who are a part of the wonderful staff at Animas Quilts and who each contributed a design for this book. They are Laura Bales, Suzanne Friend, Kim Gjere, Debbie Houser, Melinda Malone, Barbara Morgan, Jane St. Pierre, and Becky Smith. They rallied to the cry for help, jumped in, and created, getting everything done before deadlines! Additional thanks to the entire staff—their good help is what allows me the freedom to pursue writing books.

Special thanks to my husband, Jery Wyatt; daughter, Bevin Traylor; and exchange-student daughter, Miki Asai; for cooking, cleaning, and allowing quiet times to get this text prepared. They are all terrific!

And thanks to Chris Marona, my special photographer, for making us all look our best.

Credits

Editor-in-Chief .... Barbara Weiland
Managing Editor .... Greg Sharp
Technical Editor .... Ursula Reikes
Copy Editor .... Liz McGehee
Text and Cover Design .... Kay Green
Typesetting .... Kay Green
Julianna Reynolds
Photography .... Brent Kane
Chris Marona
Illustration and Graphics .... Laurel Strand

Printed in Hong Kong
98 97 96 95 94 93 6 5 4 3 2

That Patchwork Place, Inc.
PO Box 118
Bothell, WA 98041-0118
USA

Robinson, Jackie.
Animas quilts / Jackie Robinson.
p. cm.
ISBN 1-56477-037-0 :
1. Patchwork—Patterns. 2. Quilting—Patterns. I. Title.
TT835.R617 1993
746.9'7—dc20 93-25007
CIP

Table of Contents

Welcome to Animas Quilts

As visitors enter Animas Quilts and descend the steps, they see a panorama of patterns, books, and colorful quilts bathed in the overhead light of the atrium windows.

Not long ago, a woman entered our shop and at the top of the steps leading into the shop, she exclaimed, "I never dreamed I'd go down to get to Heaven!"

Animas Quilts was founded in 1988, when Jackie and her husband, Jery, moved to Durango. Jackie had started a quilt shop in the St. Louis area in 1982 and sold it in 1988 to follow their dream.

Their dream was Durango, a small town of 13,000 residents located in the southwest corner of Colorado. Founded in 1880 by the Denver and Rio Grande Railroad, the town most likely was named because of the similarity in terrain to the town of Durango, Mexico. The original settlers were mainly miners (silver) and farmers, and with the exception of Leadville, no other town in Colorado experienced as much "boom" in its growth during its first two years of existence.

Late in the 1880s, the ruins of Mesa Verde were discovered. It was several years before the value of this discovery was protected as a national park, and tourists began to come to the Four Corners region to enjoy the ruins as well as the magnificent mountains and the activities related to them.

The train continues to operate, carrying visitors to Silverton. Mesa Verde National Park attracts those interested in the history of our country before recorded time. Skiers come every winter to test their wits and knees against the slopes at Purgatory. Mountain bikers race up and down the surrounding countryside. Backpackers and hikers find trails that are free of crowds and full of beauty. Wild flowers flood the alpine valleys in the summer. Highways and byways allow motorists to see parts of the majestic beauty,

Animas Quilts stocks about thirteen hundred bolts of very special cotton fabrics in a wide array of values and colors. There's also an entire nook of solids to coordinate with any group of prints quiltmakers might put together.

The doll crafter is in paradise in this part of the store. It is filled with patterns, from primitive, to cute country, to contemporary. Our Christmas pattern tower is stocked with the "latest and greatest."

while four-wheel-drive roads lead into some incredibly scenic areas. Durango is a dream come true.

Animas Quilts is named after the river that both meanders and rampages through the town of Durango. Its complete name is El Rio de las Animas Perdidas, Spanish for "the river of lost souls." While quilters are certainly not lost, their souls are lost in their art; thus, the name fits.

Originally located in the front part of Jery's garden center, Animas Quilts moved to downtown Durango in 1989, then again in 1990 to its present location on the northeast corner of Sixth and Main. At one time, that corner housed a gasoline station, and when they removed the underground tanks, they kept digging and excavated the area the shop now fills. With atrium windows on the north and east, the shop has lots of light illuminating the walls lined with quilts. (Don't worry—the windows have been treated to cut down on the ultraviolet rays, and the quilts are protected!)

From the street level, what you see are lots of quilts, dolls, patterns, and books to tempt quilters and crafters alike. Just inside the door is a landing, with steps leading down to the quilters' paradise. Once at the base of the steps, you're treated to more quilts and dolls, along with tools to make quilting easier. There is a sewing area with chairs and magazines to hold the interest of spouses, and enough quilts on display in a variety of patterns and colors to allow everyone who visits to find something they like. In addition to a wide variety of colorful quilting fabrics from the United States, we also import a wonderful fabric from Holland. The Bou BouDima line features beautiful wax resist and Java prints on 100% cotton. They have a wonderful hand and are fun to work into quilts!

The overhead windows are not the only things that keep Animas Quilts light and airy. We have lots of fun activities happening every year. Each April we head out of town for a weekend quilting retreat. Beginning on Friday evening, we have a get-acquainted show-and-tell, followed by the first quilt lesson of the weekend. Saturday brings more new quilts to experience and

This special cotton fabric with a wonderful hand, called Bou BouDima, is imported from Holland. Its bold and dramatic designs are wonderful accents to any quilt. The collection includes Java and wax prints. Ordering information is on page 88.

From left to right: Laura Bales, Kristie Nicholls, Britt Toppenberg, Sue Ann Shwiller, Joan DiBlasi, Melinda Malone, Kim Gjere, Suzanne Friend, Jane St. Pierre, Becky Smith, Barbara Morgan, and Jackie Robinson. Not pictured: Debbie Houser.

enjoy, and usually some sort of surprise. We continue on Sunday with another quilt lesson. The entire weekend is always great fun for our quilting friends because, as we all know, quilters are the "best" people.

During the summer we try to have a staff barbeque for couples. Enjoying the friendships fostered in the shop, it's fun to get to know everyone's "other half."

In the fall we import quilting instructors from all over the country and host weekend seminars with these special people.

Animas Quilts looks forward to your visit, and we know you'll find the shop and the scenic Durango area worth visiting.

Meet Jackie Robinson

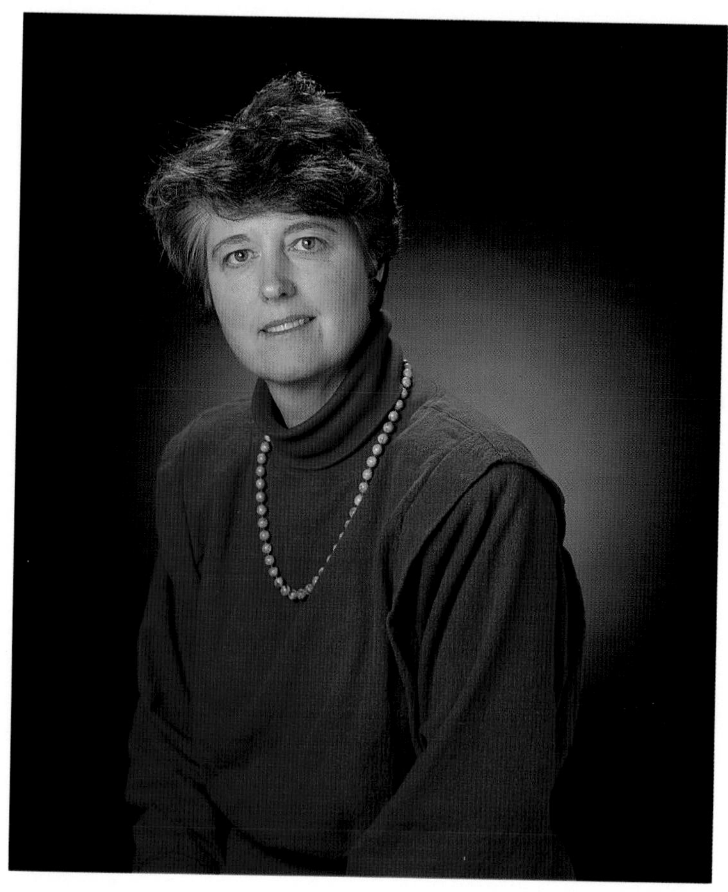

Jackie Robinson considers herself to be one of the luckiest people in the world, as she manages to earn a living doing exactly what she likes best—designing quilts and helping others to do the same. She sometimes wonders how she could be so fortunate to have had the opportunity to begin not one, but two quilt shops—both of them successful—and what possessed her to tackle the amount of work it takes to begin a business—twice!

With a degree in fashion merchandising, Jackie worked as a department-store buyer until it was time for a family. Her two children are son, Serge Traylor (21), and daughter, Bevin Traylor (18), neither of whom likes to sew, but can.

In 1983 Jackie met and married Jery Wyatt, a liberated and gentle man, who didn't mind that she didn't want to change her name again. He swings a mighty hammer, which is a wonderful asset for a quilt-shop husband.

Jackie's first book, *Chains of Love,* was published in 1988. Since then, she's written several more, and in 1991 started a small publishing company of her own.

Lately, she's been enjoying an opportunity to study Frank Lloyd Wright (1867–1959), one of America's most impressive architects. With the permission of the Frank Lloyd Wright Foundation, she's working to develop some of his designs into patchwork. This is one of the special classes Jackie offers when traveling and teaching. In addition, she has recently designed a special tool to help you mark mitered corners on your quilt bindings. For more information, see page 21.

General Directions

Preparing Fabric

Tools to have within arm's reach as you sew:

Iron and ironing board
Seam ripper (ounce of prevention . . .)
Pencil & paper (It's your prerogative to change the design.)
Ruler
Remote control for the TV
Phone

Always select quality fabrics. We recommend 42"- to 44"-wide, 100% cotton fabrics, and our market is full of a wonderful selection of these. Fabrics available in quilt shops and fine fabric stores are usually first-run fabrics, and shrinkage is really a minimal concern. Just the same, it's always a good idea to pretreat your fabrics to prevent any surprises.

To pretreat cotton fabric, wash it in warm water without detergent, as the detergent carries the sizing away, too. Then, dry in a dryer and press. After pressing, refold it as it came off the bolt, lining up the selvages so they are parallel and matching.

Pretreating is also your protection against colors that run or bleed onto their neighbor. Some deep-color dyes are simply harder than others to "set." If you get a tinted or colored rinse, chances are you have an unstable dye in your fabric. These can be set by adding salt or white vinegar to the water and soaking. White vinegar usually works the best and the quickest, but obviously, when you press it later, the aroma is sometimes a bit much! So, we usually try the salt first. Add at least ½ pound of salt to a low-water load of cold water in your washer and stir until dissolved. Add the fabric and let it soak overnight, if possible. Rinse, and hope the rinse water is clear. If not, repeat. Likewise, for the white vinegar, put at least ½ pint into a low-water tub of cold water and stir. It usually takes only a couple of these special rinses to "set" the colors. Dry and press.

Yardage for our quilts is based on quality 44"-wide cotton fabrics. After the minimum amounts are determined, we add 10% (3% for shrinkage and 7% for a "goof" factor). For backing yardage, we add only the 3% for maximum shrinkage, as we really doubt that you'll make a cutting error there.

Rotary Cutting

All of the patterns included in this book are planned for rotary cutting. We've found that accuracy increases as the length of the cut decreases. Therefore, we suggest that you fold your fabric in fourths before beginning to cut.

1. Place the selvage edges together, keeping them parallel and also keeping the center fold of the fabric smooth and unbuckled.
2. Pick up the center fold and place it on top of the parallel selvage edges so the width of your fabric is folded down to about 11".

3. Use a rotary cutter and a ruler to make the first cut along the edge of the fabric. Line up one of the cross lines on the ruler with the folded edge of the fabric so this first cut is perfectly straight. (If it isn't, your strips will not be straight—they'll be stretched-out W's.)

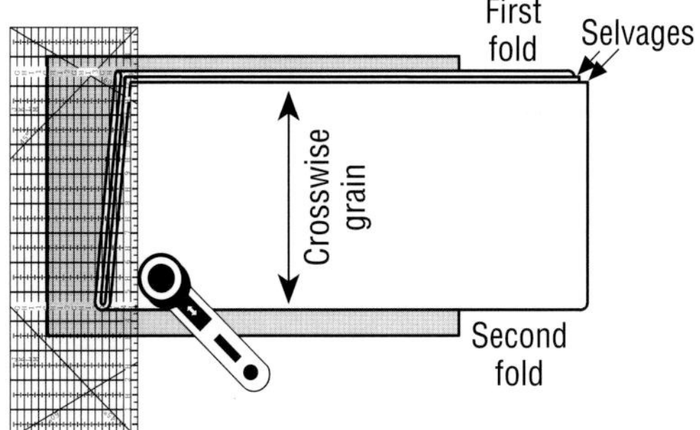

4. Place the appropriate grid line on the ruler along the cut edge of the folded fabric and cut the subsequent strips.

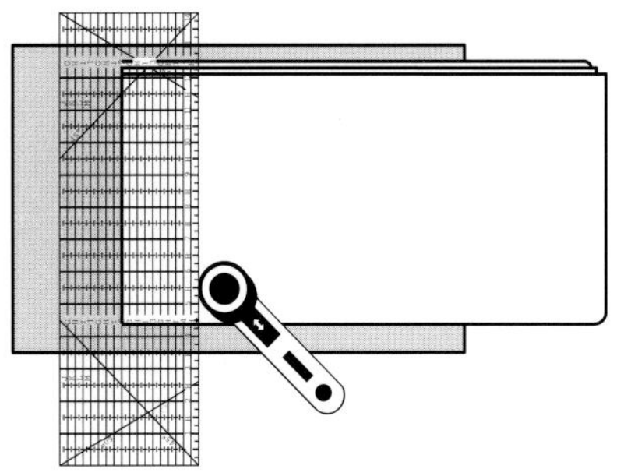

Preparing to Sew

The patterns are designed to be made using ¼"-wide seam allowances. Many quilters simply use the outer right-hand edge of their sewing-machine presser foot as a ¼" guide. If it is not a true ¼", pieces will not fit correctly, and the end result will be a puckered quilt, which is either too big for the backing or too small for the bed.

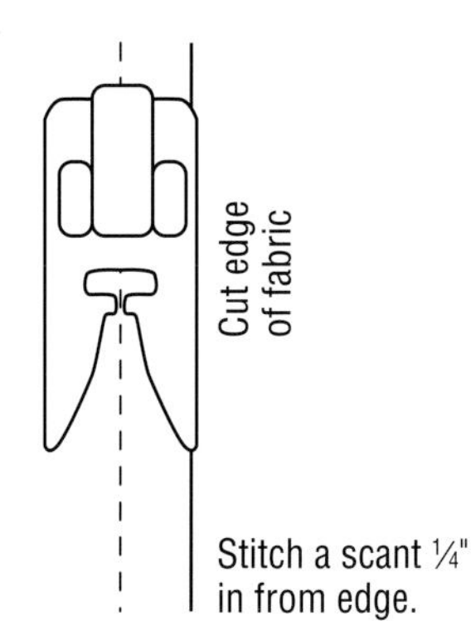

Accuracy in your ¼"-wide seam allowances is really important. Take a few minutes to establish it and find a way to mark your machine if necessary, so you'll stay on a ¼"-wide seam allowance.

Actually, my ¼"-wide seam allowance is about two threads of fabric scant of a true ¼". When I press, the fold of the press takes up those two threads and my seam allowance is perfect. This slightly scant ¼"-wide seam allowance is the one we recommend.

It is best to use 100% cotton thread for piecing quilts made of 100% cotton fabric, because you want the thread holding your quilt together to be the same strength as the fabric. If you used polyester thread or cotton-covered poly, it would be stronger than the fabric, and the stronger polyester thread could cut through the fibers of the cotton quilt if it received some strain. However, if the quilt were stitched with 100% cotton thread, chances are the threads would break or pop under stress instead of cutting the fabric. We never like to think about the possibility of having to mend a quilt someday, but it is a real probability that our grandchildren will inherit our treasures and need to do some repairs.

Place your machine within arms' reach of your ironing board if possible. I've seen several wonderful sewing rooms, and the one thing they have in common is easy access to the iron. You need to press as you go, and if it's close by, you'll be more apt to press often. The key word here is *press,* not iron. The verb "iron" implies sliding on the fabric, which can distort quilt blocks in a hurry. "Press," on the other hand, means to place the heavy heat on the quilt block, then lift and replace. Always press; never iron.

Sewing Strip Sets

When sewing a strip set, if you sew several strips together in the same direction, chances are your strip set will be curved when finished. In order to keep strip sets straight, we suggest antidirectional stitching. This means that you sew the second strip to the first strip, keeping the second strip on top. Then sew the third strip to the second, again keeping the second strip on top. To do this, you'll need to begin at the bottom of the strip set. As the fourth strip is added to the first three, the fourth strip will be on top of the third. Continue in this fashion until all required strips have been added.

Keep even-numbered strips on top of odd-numbered ones when sewing.

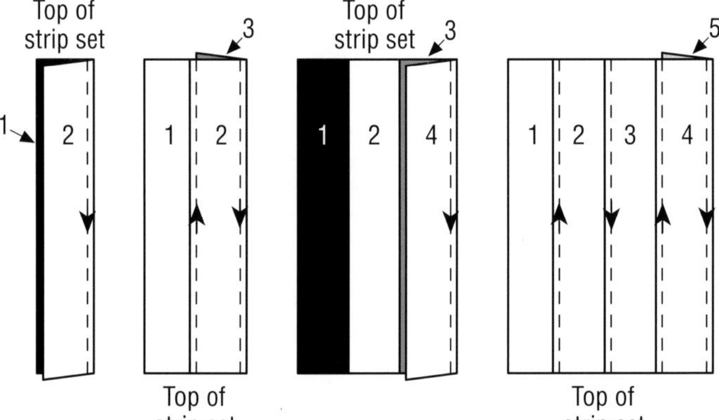

Antidirectional stitching places an equal amount of stretch on both edges of any strip, which in turn keeps each individual strip straight, and therefore keeps the entire strip set straight!

Making Half-Square Triangle Units

There are lots of methods for creating half-square triangle units. Some methods are better than others, so we'll outline our favorites here. You may even have a different method that you prefer. Whatever method you select, remember that each square yields two half-square triangle units.

Drawing a Grid

This is an easy method to make half-square triangles.

1. Place the two selected fabrics, right sides together, and press. (This helps them stick together.) On the wrong side of the lightest one, draw a grid of squares, making the squares ⅞" larger than the finished measurement of the half-square triangle units you need.

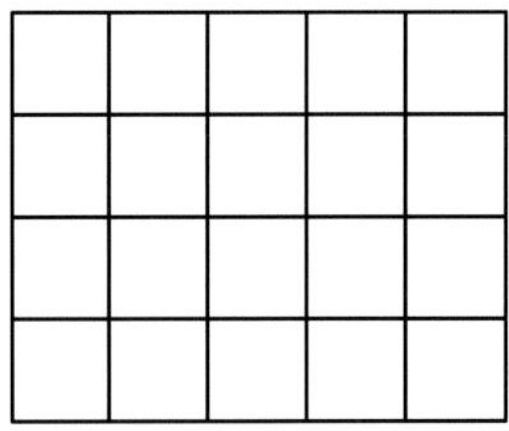

2. Begin in the upper left corner and draw a line diagonally through a row of squares, taking care that the drawn lines intersect exactly in the corners. Then skip a block and draw another diagonal line in the same direction. Continue drawing diagonal lines through every second row of blocks. Then, draw lines going the opposite direction in the remaining blocks. If you draw these diagonals in alternating rows of squares, you will be able to sew a continuous line around the grid.

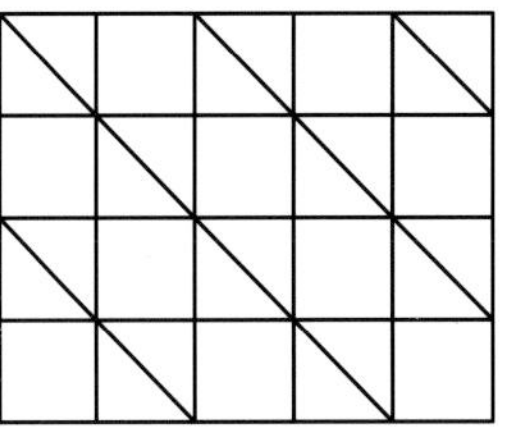

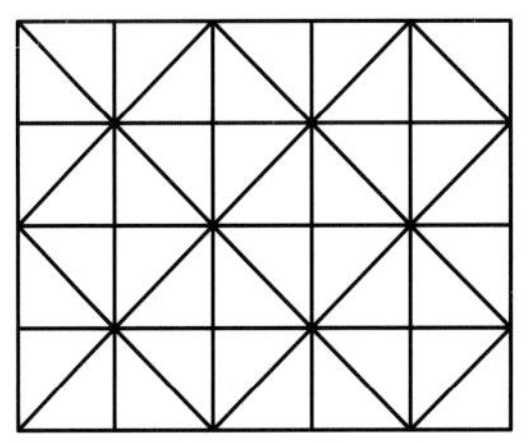

3. Pin fabrics together. Using an accurate ¼"-wide seam allowance, stitch ¼" to each side of the drawn lines.

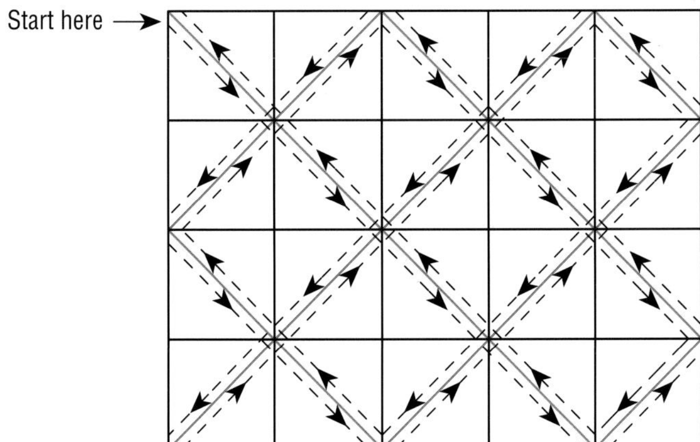

4. Cut apart on all the straight and diagonal lines and press seams toward the darker fabric.

Using Speed Grids®

The Speed Grid is a transparent grid stencil for speed-piecing half-square triangle blocks. Speed Grids come in ½", 1", 2", and 3" finished sizes.

1. Place the two selected fabrics, right sides together, and press. Position the Speed Grid on the wrong side of the lightest fabrics and draw through the stencil lines.
2. Pin fabrics together and stitch on the diagonal lines you've traced.
3. Cut apart on the vertical and horizontal lines, and between the diagonal stitching lines. Press seams toward the darker fabric.

Using Preprinted Grid Paper

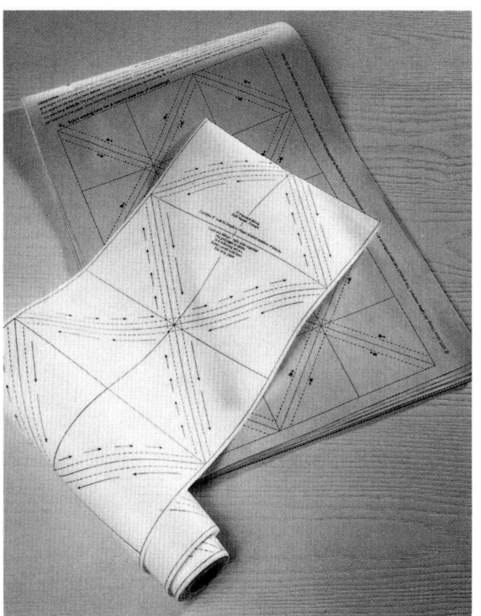

This is our personal favorite because it's quick and practically "goof-proof." This paper is preprinted with squares and diagonal stitching lines and comes in 1", 1½", 2", 2½", and 3" finished sizes. They are wonderful and they are accurate.

1. Place the two selected fabrics right sides together and press.
2. Position the preprinted paper on the back side of the layered fabric and pin in place.
3. Stitch on the diagonal lines, following the arrows, using a very short stitch length to help perforate the paper.
4. Cut apart on the vertical and horizontal lines, and between the stitching lines.
5. Gently remove the paper and press the seams toward the darker fabric.

Cutting Individual Squares

This method is best when you only need a few half-square triangle units, but you need several different combinations.

1. From the selected fabrics, cut squares ⅞" larger than the desired finished size.
2. Layer the fabrics, right sides together, and draw a diagonal line on the wrong side of the lightest fabric.
3. Stitch ¼" to each side of the diagonal line and cut apart on the line. Press seams toward the darker fabric and trim the "dog-ear" corners.

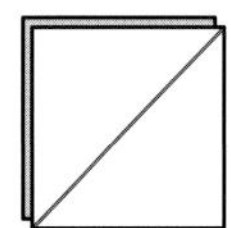
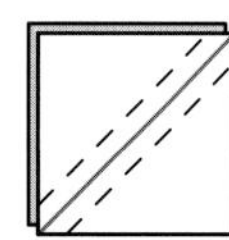
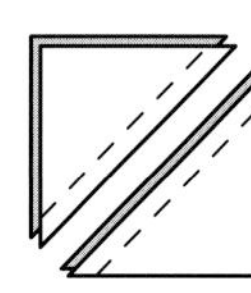
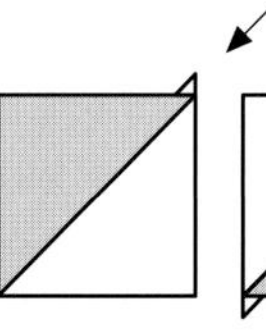

You can use a tool called a Quick Quarter® to make this process even easier. It is precisely ½" wide, with a slit in the center to use for exact diagonal placement on the square. Center the Quick Quarter on the wrong side of the layered squares and draw next to its base on both sides to mark the stitching lines. Stitch, cut apart, and press seams toward the darker fabric.

Making Quarter-Square Triangle Units

1. Make half-square triangle units (as shown above) from a grid that is 1¼" larger than the finished size.
2. Place two of these special half-square triangle units right sides together and with opposite colors of fabrics together; that is, place the dark part of the half-square triangle unit directly over the light part of the other half-square triangle unit.
3. On the wrong side of the layered fabric pair, draw a new diagonal line that is perpendicular to the previously stitched seam. (Or, use the Quick Quarter to mark stitching lines as shown above.)
4. Sew ¼" to each side of this new diagonal line; cut apart.

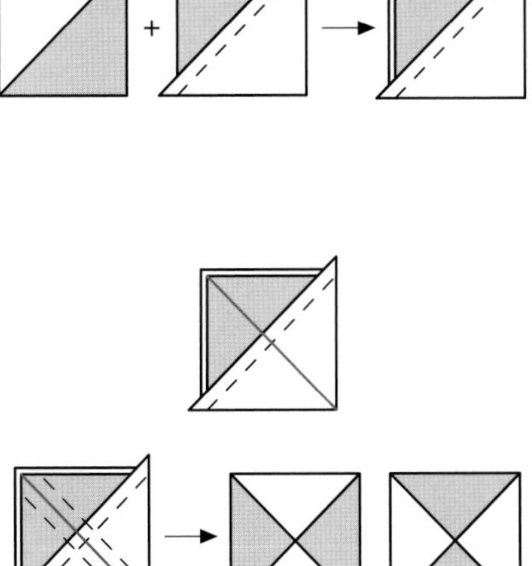

Assembling the Quilt Top

Once all the blocks for a quilt are made and it's time to stitch them together into a quilt top, we've found this one technique to be the best. If your blocks are not all exactly the same size (perish the thought!), this method will solve assembly problems. Perhaps you've sewn blocks together in rows, then attached the rows together only to discover the vertical seams didn't match up. This method will solve that problem. We call it "Pairs of Pairs of Pairs."

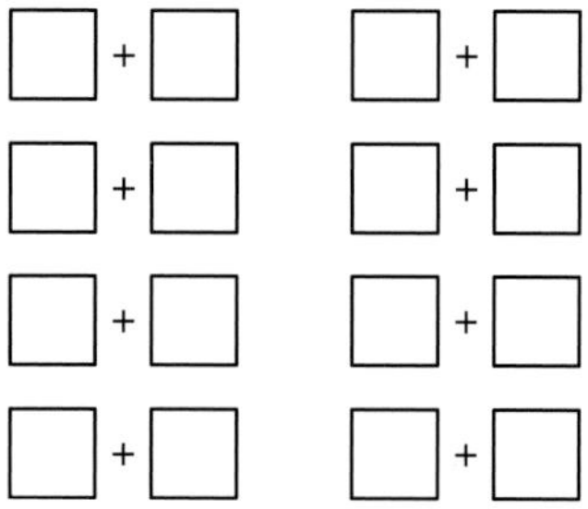

1. Arrange the blocks, following the quilt plan provided with each quilt.
2. Begin by sewing the blocks into "pairs" with vertical seams. Do not press seams yet. 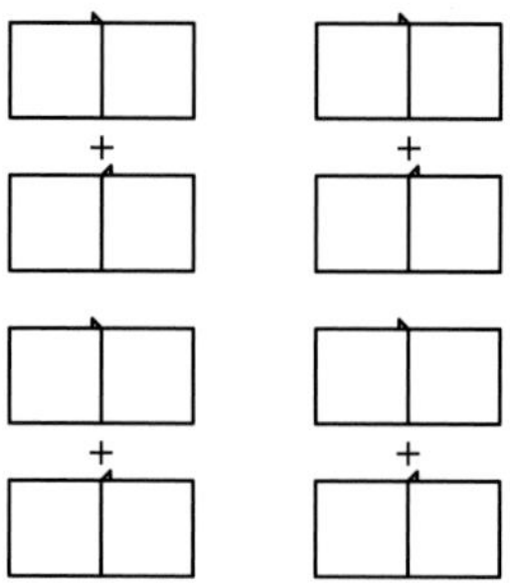
3. Stitch "pairs of pairs" together with horizontal seams, alternating the direction of the seams that you cross. Each time you cross seams for the first time, send the two meeting seams in opposite directions, taking care as you progress through assembly to maintain the direction you've already sent a seam. 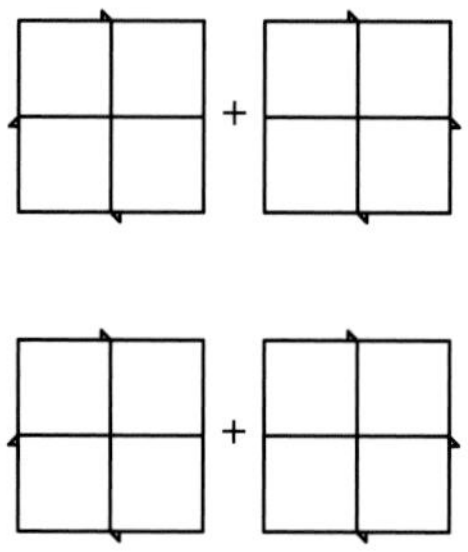
4. Stitch "pairs of pairs of pairs" together with vertical seams, again alternating the directions of the crossed seams. 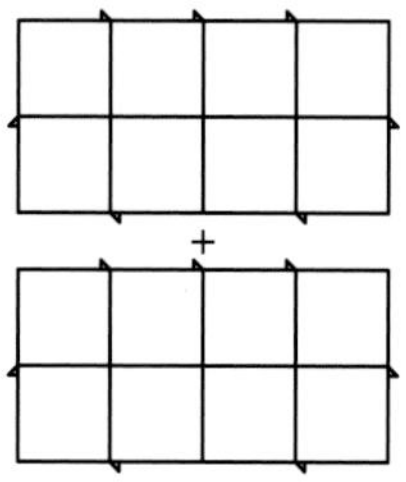
5. Stitch "pairs of pairs of pairs of pairs" together with horizontal seams, and so on. When blocks or units of blocks are not all the same size, match them at each seam and adjust toward the smaller block.

The direction of the stitching will constantly alternate. Eventually, you'll have it all assembled into a few large chunks. At this moment, it's a good time to press before stitching the final few seams. This assembly process really works, and it makes for flat quilt tops.

Attaching Borders

1. Cut strips for borders across the fabric width (crosswise grain). Sew the strips together end to end when extra length is needed. Trim off the selvages when joining seams and press the seams open.
2. The best way to measure for borders is to place the border strips on top of the flat quilt top, in the center of the quilt. Measure the length for the side borders first. Cut borders to fit; then sew, easing if necessary. Measure the width for the top and bottom borders, including the side borders. Cut borders to fit; then sew, easing if necessary.

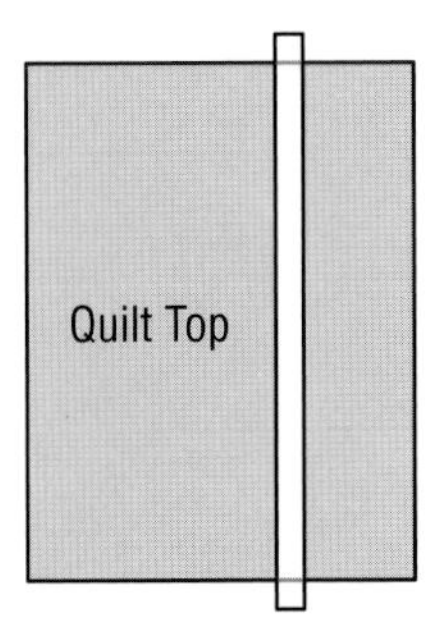

Measuring for side borders

Note: You may find that you need to ease the border to one edge of the quilt but not to the other, due to stretching or inaccuracies in stitching. This is normal. Cutting border strips to match the measurements at the center of the quilt ensures that your quilt top will be "square," without ripples or wavy edges, after you have attached the borders.

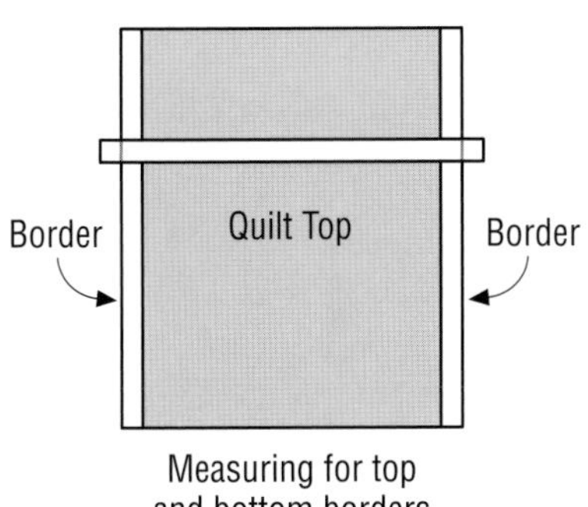

Measuring for top and bottom borders

Straight-Cut Borders

1. Measure and cut two side borders.
2. Pin in place, easing as necessary, and stitch.
3. Press the seams toward the border.
4. Measure and cut two borders for the top and bottom edges.
5. Pin in place, easing as necessary, and stitch.
6. Press the seams toward the border.

Repeat this process for each additional border.

Mitered Borders

This is the method I prefer for making mitered corners in quilt borders. It ensures that you always have enough length on each border strip to make a 45° miter.

1. Add ½" to the width of the border strip. For example, to a 3"-wide border, add ½" to total 3½".
2. From the end of the border strip, measure the amount determined in step 1, to create a "tail," and place a pin.

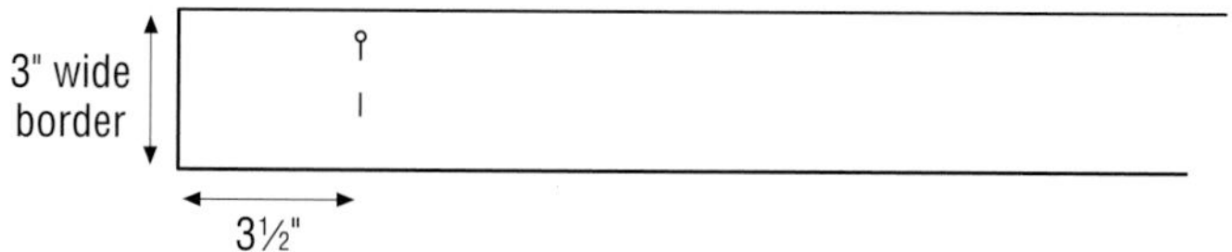

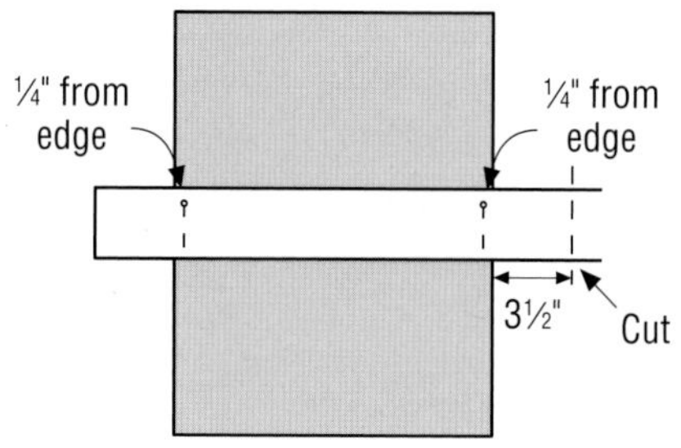

3. Place the border across the quilt top and position the pin ¼" in from one edge of the quilt top, at the center where you're measuring for the proper length. Place another pin in the border strip, ¼" in from the opposite edge of the quilt top.

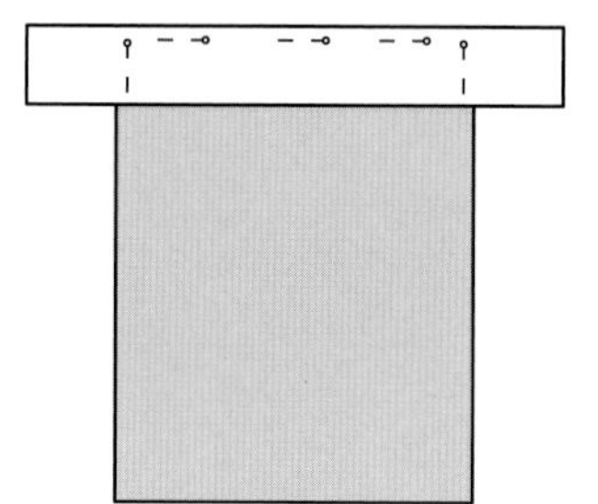

4. Cut the border strip after leaving another "tail" the same size as the first one (3½" in our example). Cut two strips the same length; mark the ¼" seam placement and pin in place along the edge of the quilt, easing as necessary.

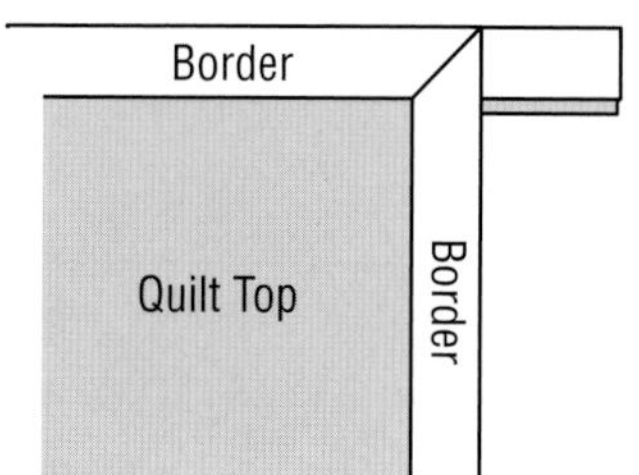

5. Stitch from one ¼" pin mark to the other ¼" pin mark at the opposite end.
6. Repeat steps 1–5 for the remaining borders. Press the seams toward the border.
7. Lay the first corner to be mitered on the ironing board. Fold under the border strip that is perpendicular to the ironing board, placing its "tail" on top of the border that is parallel to the ironing board and matching the inside edges of the border strip (the one that has been stitched to the quilt). You'll be able to tell when this looks right.

8. Press the fold and pin to hold the two border strips together.
9. Gently fold back the top layer and stitch in the crease.
10. When you are satisfied that it looks right, trim excess fabric away to a ¼"-wide seam allowance and press seams open. Repeat for each corner.

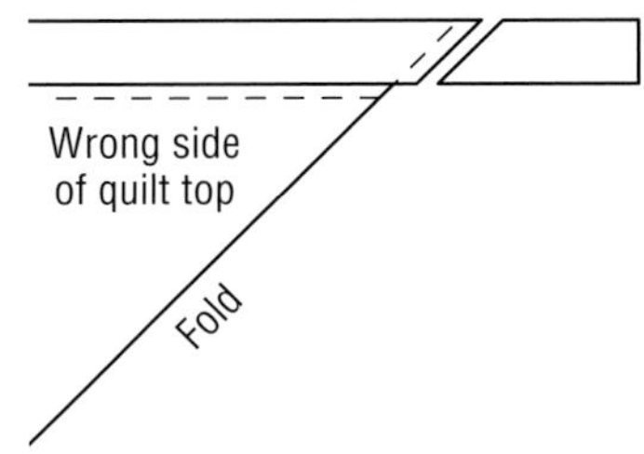

Backing

Piecing diagrams for backing are given at the bottom of the yardage charts. They indicate how the backing should be pieced to fit the required quilt size. Measure the length and width of the quilt top before cutting backing; then cut backing 4" larger than the quilt top in length and width. For pieced backings, place seams down the middle of the back of the quilt, or to one side, whichever you prefer.

Directional fabrics that must be matched will require more fabric than the yardage given for each quilt.

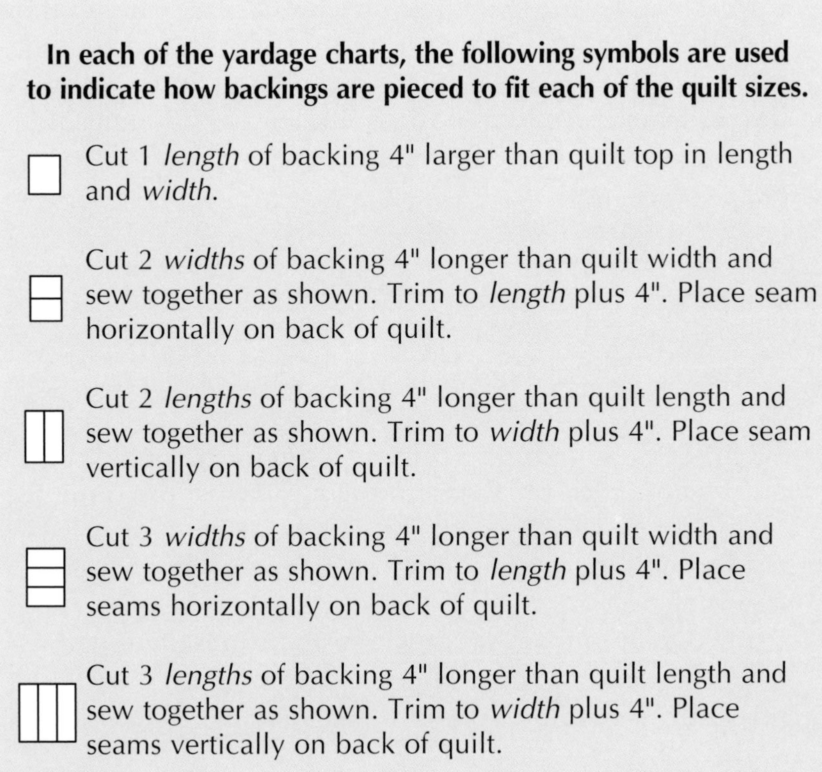

In each of the yardage charts, the following symbols are used to indicate how backings are pieced to fit each of the quilt sizes.

Cut 1 *length* of backing 4" larger than quilt top in length and *width.*

Cut 2 *widths* of backing 4" longer than quilt width and sew together as shown. Trim to *length* plus 4". Place seam horizontally on back of quilt.

Cut 2 *lengths* of backing 4" longer than quilt length and sew together as shown. Trim to *width* plus 4". Place seam vertically on back of quilt.

Cut 3 *widths* of backing 4" longer than quilt width and sew together as shown. Trim to *length* plus 4". Place seams horizontally on back of quilt.

Cut 3 *lengths* of backing 4" longer than quilt length and sew together as shown. Trim to *width* plus 4". Place seams vertically on back of quilt.

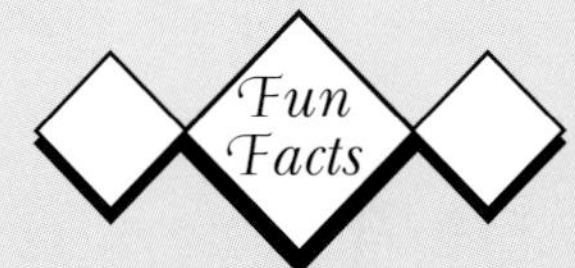

You'll get a rhythm going to music, and soon you'll be done, and happy too! Our "favorite quilting music" is:

Natalie Cole (so you can sing along)

Bach (to keep you relaxed)

Mozart (for speeding up)

Gershwin (you've got rhythm)

Piano music of all sorts (gives you that shopping mall feeling)

Quilting

Probably the most personal part of quilt construction is the quilting method selected. We are primarily machine quilters but maintain the greatest respect for hand quilting. Fortunately, techniques for machine quilting have improved so we can accomplish more quality quilts in our lifetimes. Quilting suggestions are provided for each quilt. After quilting, leave about ½" of backing and batting extending beyond the top of your quilt when you trim.

Binding

For strength and durability, we use a double-fold binding in our quilts.

1. Cut binding strips 3" wide from the fabric width (crosswise grain).
2. If necessary, sew strips together, end to end, to make binding strips long enough for each side of the quilt top. Press strips in half lengthwise with wrong sides together.
3. Using a ¼"-wide seam allowance, sew binding to the quilt through all layers, matching the raw edges of the binding with the raw edges of the quilt top. (Batting and backing will extend beyond the quilt edges.) Begin and end stitching ¼" from the edges of the quilt, leaving 1½" tails of binding at both ends. Sew the binding strips to all four edges of the quilt.

4. To miter the binding so it turns a square corner and is mitered on both the front and back sides of the quilt, fold the quilt at a corner so the two adjacent binding strips are stacked one on top of the other. Pin carefully to hold them together.
5. Use a pencil to mark a dot where the stitching ended at the ¼" seam allowance. Then, use a ruler and mark a dot across from the first dot, on the fold of the binding.

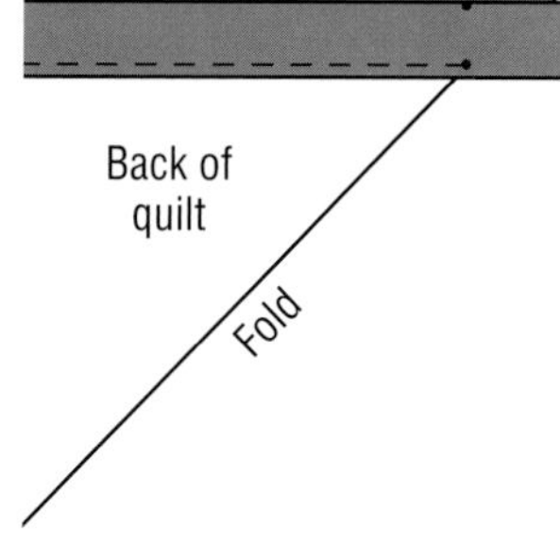

6. Place the point of the corner edge of your ruler toward the "tails" of the binding, and in between the two dots as shown. Draw a line from dot to dot, going around the 90° corner.

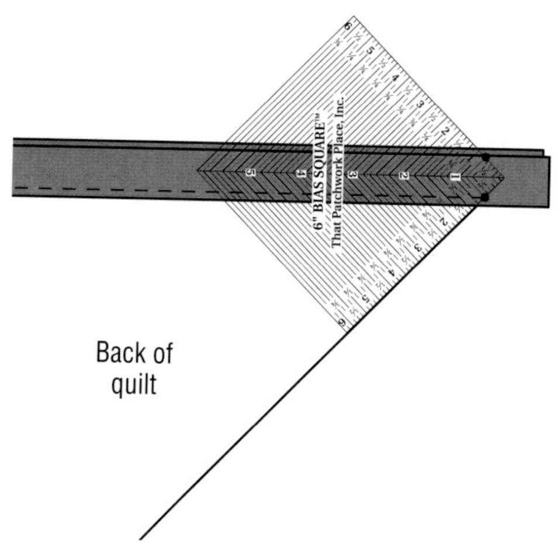

7. Stitch on the marked line and trim away the excess binding fabric beyond the corner.
8. Carefully turn the binding right side out. The extra ½" of batting and backing you left on your quilt will pack into the binding to make it strong. Blindstitch the binding on the back side of the quilt.

Note: We now offer a new tool designed to make it easy to mark a perfect double miter on your quilt binding. The "Binding Miter Tool" has the four angles most commonly used by quilters—60°, 90°, 120°, and 135°. See page 88 to order this tool.

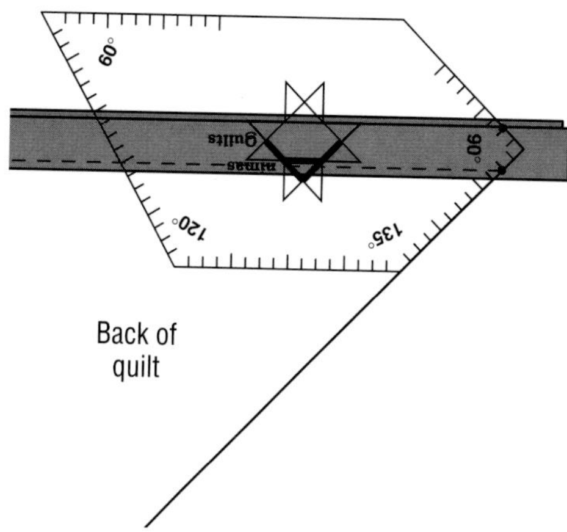

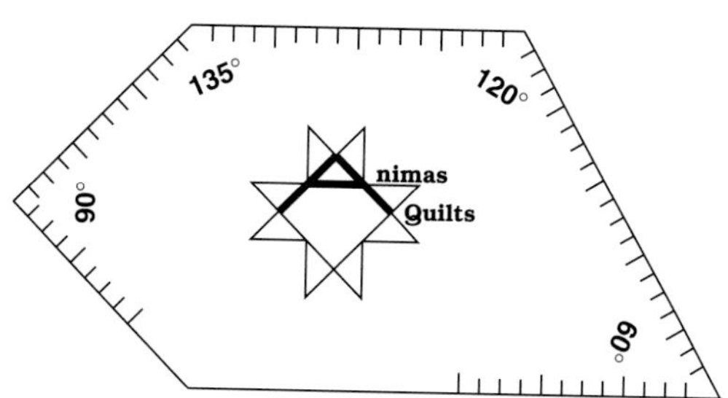

Labeling Your Quilt

Make a label for your quilt that includes the name of the quilt, your name, and the date you finished it. If it is a gift, put the name of the recipient on it, too, and anything else that strikes your fancy, such as a favorite quote or sentiment.

We hope that you'll enjoy making the quilts in this book and that you'll be inspired to create your own quilts. We always love quilt pictures and show-and-tell. If you'll send us a photo of your quilt made from one of these patterns, we'll keep it in our special gallery and send you a small token of our appreciation.

Durango Skies Are Laced with Stars

by Jackie Robinson

Alpine meadows surround our town in places that are really not difficult to reach. Usually, you can expect the wild flowers to be at their peak in mid-July, and they remain excitingly colorful through August.

Imagine camping in this meadow on a summer night, the sky crystal clear and deep blue, and the stars dancing across the heavens, speaking to the blooms below. That's living!

Durango Skies Are Laced with Stars, by Jackie Robinson, 1992, Durango, Colorado, 81½" x 111½".

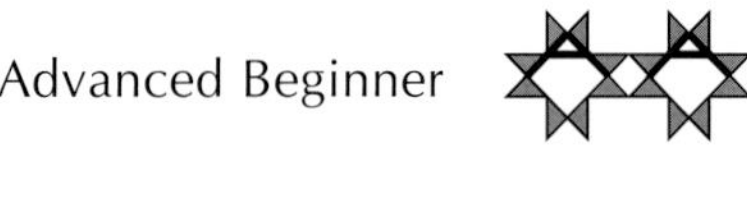

Crib/Lap Twin Double/Queen King

Crib/Lap

Twin

Double/Queen/King

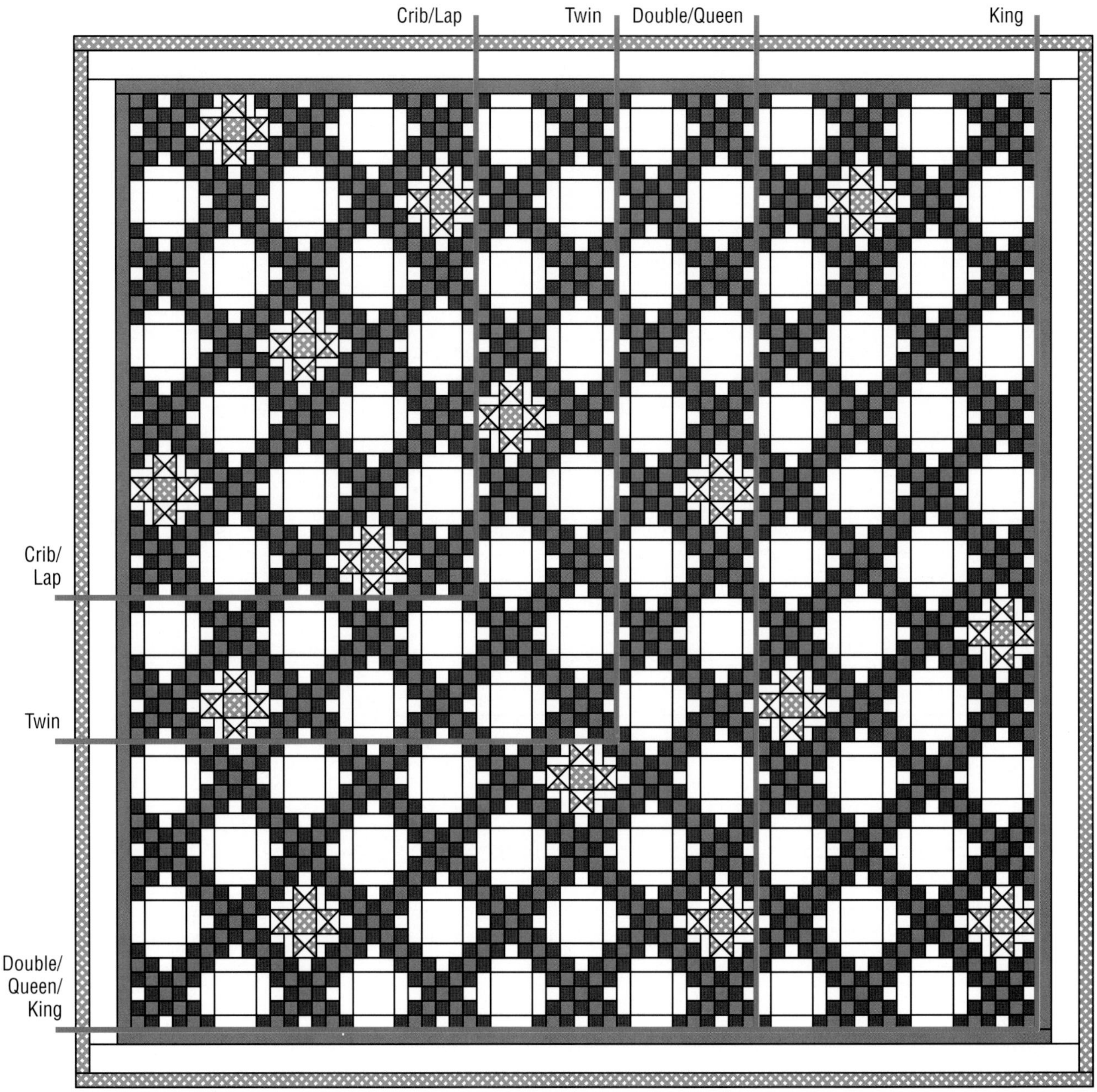

Quilt Plan

QUILT SIZES

Crib/Lap	*Twin*	*Dbl/Q*	*King*
Finished Size	**Finished Size**	**Finished Size**	**Finished Size**
51½" x 66½"	66½" x 96½"	81½" x 111½"	111½" x 111½"
No. of Blocks	**No. of Blocks**	**No. of Blocks**	**No. of Blocks**
35	63	117	169
Block Layout	**Block Layout**	**Block Layout**	**Block Layout**
5 x 7	7 x 9	9 x 13	13 x 13

Number of Blocks

	Crib/Lap	Twin	Dbl/Q	King
Block A	18	32	59	85
Block B	14	26	48	69
Star Block	3	5	10	15

Block Size: 7½"

Block A

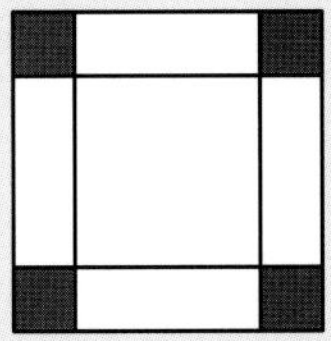

Block B

Star Block

Color Key

A (double chain)

B (center chain)

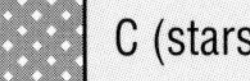

C (stars)

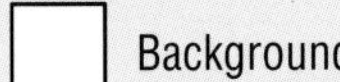

Background

MATERIALS: 44"-wide fabric

Purchase the required yardage for the quilt size you are making.

Fabric Requirements in Yards

	Crib/Lap	Twin	Dbl/Q	King
A (double chain)	1⅛	2	3	4½
B (center chain)	⅝	1⅛	1⅔	2½
C (stars)	¼	¼	⅜	⅝
Background	1⅜	2⅓	3⅔	5½
Inner Border	⅓	½	½	⅝
Middle Border	⅞	1⅛	1¼	1½
Outer Border	⅜	½	⅝	⅔
Binding	⅝	¾	1	1
Backing	3¼	5¾	6⅔	10
Piecing for Backing				

Directions

Cut all strips across the width of the fabric (crosswise grain).

Block A

1. Cut 2"-wide strips from Fabrics A, B, and the background as shown in the chart below. Remember to cut accurately!

Fabric	Number of Strips: Crib/Lap	Twin	Dbl/Q	King
A (double chain)	12	24	36	55
B (center chain)	9	18	27	41
Background	4	8	12	19

2. Assemble strip sets as shown in the piecing diagram below, using a scant ¼"-wide seam and antidirectional stitching (page 12). Press seams toward Fabric B and the background; crosscut into 2"-wide segments. See chart below for the number of strips sets and number of 2" segments required for the size you are making.

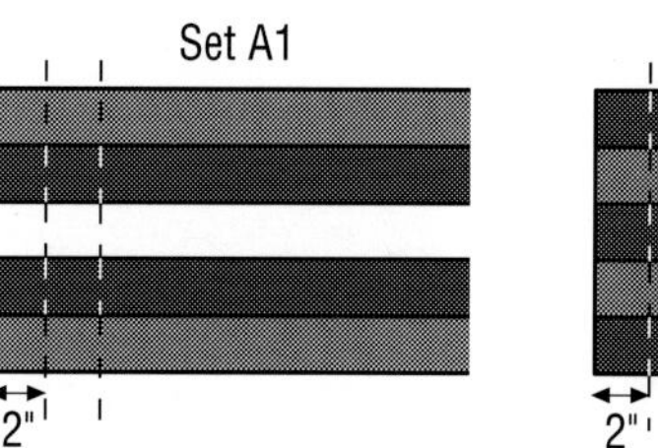

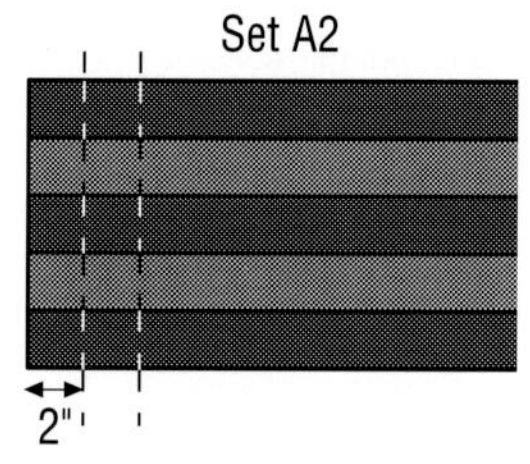

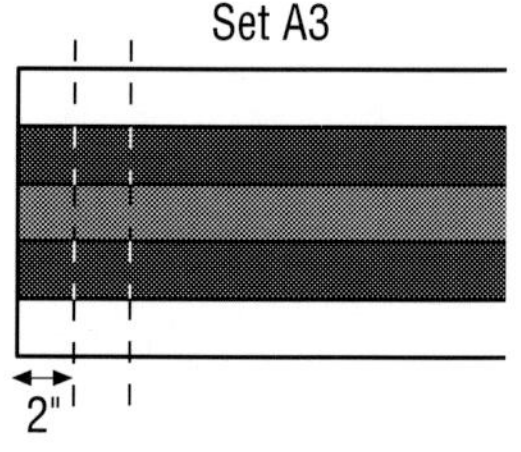

Number of Strip Sets and Segments

Block A Strip Sets	*Crib/Lap* Strip Sets	*Crib/Lap* 2" Segments	*Twin* Strip Sets	*Twin* 2" Segments	*Dbl/Q* Strip Sets	*Dbl/Q* 2" Segments	*King* Strip Sets	*King* 2" Segments
A1	2	36	4	64	6	118	9	170
A2	2	36	4	64	6	118	9	170
A3	1	18	2	32	3	59	5	85

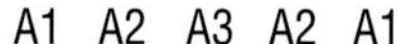

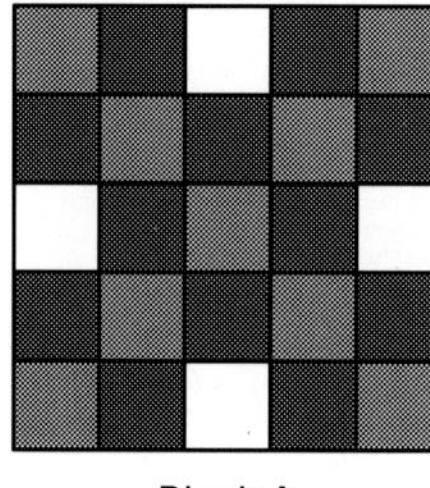

Block A

3. Assemble the 2" segments as shown to make the required number of Block A. Press seams toward Fabric B and the background.

Block B

1. Cut 2"- and 5"-wide strips from Fabric A and the background as shown in the chart below.

Fabric	*Strip Width*	Number of Strips: *Crib/Lap*	*Twin*	*Dbl/Q*	*King*
A (double chain)	2"	4	6	10	14
Background	2"	4	8	12	18
Background	5"	4	7	11	16

2. Assemble strip sets, following the piecing diagram on page 27, using a scant ¼"-wide seam and antidirectional stitching (page 12). Press seams toward the background fabric. Cut 2"-wide segments from B1 strip sets, and 5"-wide segments from B2 strip sets. See chart at top of page 27.

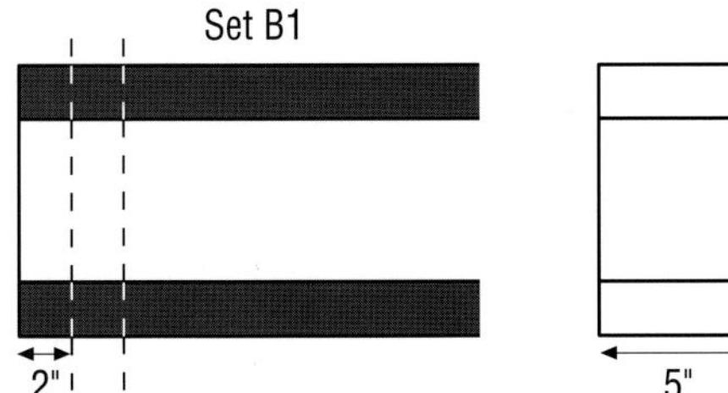

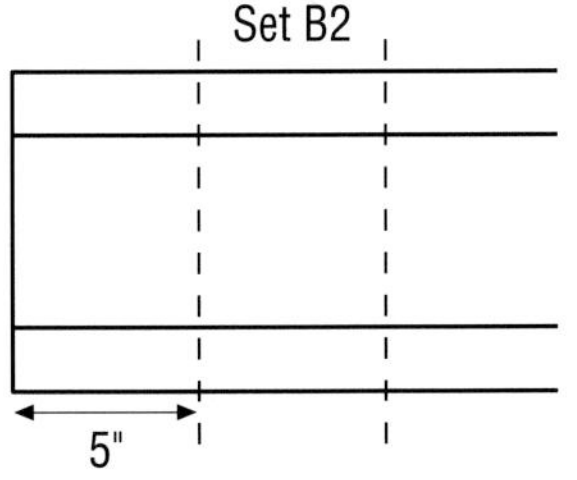

Number of Strip Sets and Segments

Block B Strip Sets	Segment Width	*Crib/Lap* Strip Sets	*Crib/Lap* Segments	*Twin* Strip Sets	*Twin* Segments	*Dbl/Q* Strip Sets	*Dbl/Q* Segments	*King* Strip Sets	*King* Segments
B1	2"	2	28	3	52	5	96	7	138
B2	5"	2	14	4	26	6	48	9	69

3. Assemble the segments as shown to make the required number of Block B. Press the seams toward the background.

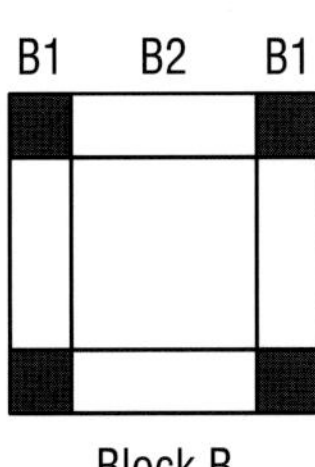

Block B

Star Block

You're almost done. The Star blocks remain to be made, and they are lots of fun! A Star block is a three-patch block, and we'll build it in sections, then put it together. See chart below.

Star Block Sections	Number of Sections *Crib/Lap*	*Twin*	*Dbl/Q*	*King*
Corner Units	12	20	40	60
Star Points	12	20	40	60
Centers	3	5	10	15

Corner Units

1. Cut strips from Fabric A and the background as shown below.

Fabric	*Strip Width*	Number of Strips *Crib/Lap*	*Twin*	*Dbl/Q*	*King*
A (double chain)	2"	1	1	2	3
Background	1½"	2	3	6	8

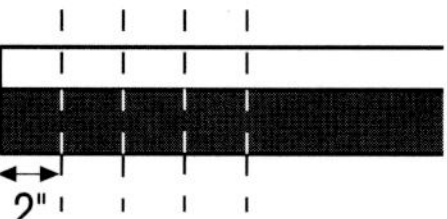

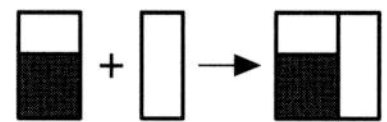

2. Sew strips of Fabric A and the background together. The number of strip sets you'll need is equal to the number of 2" strips cut from Fabric A. Press the seam toward the background. Crosscut the strip sets into 2"-wide segments.
3. Cut the remaining 1½"-wide background strips into 3" lengths and attach to the 2"-wide segments as shown to complete the corner units.

Star Point Units

1. Star point units are created from Fabric C and the background fabric, with 1 piece of each needed for every 2 units. Cut 3¾"-wide strips from Fabric C and the background; then crosscut each strip to create 3¾" x 3¾" squares. See chart below.

Number of Strips and Squares

Fabric	*Crib/Lap* Strips	*Crib/Lap* Squares	*Twin* Strips	*Twin* Squares	*Dbl/Q* Strips	*Dbl/Q* Squares	*King* Strips	*King* Squares
C (star)	1	6	1	10	2	20	3	30
Background	1	6	1	10	2	20	3	30

2. Place 3¾" squares of Fabric C and background together, with right sides facing. Use a pencil to draw a diagonal line on the wrong side of the lighter fabric. Stitch ¼" away from this line, on both sides of the line. Cut along the line. Press seams toward the darker fabric and trim the "dog-ear" corners.

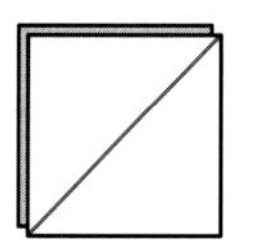
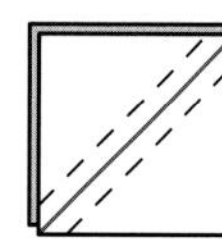

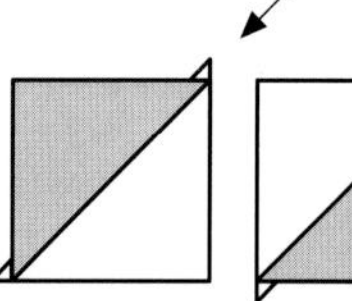

The Quick Quarter speeds this up. (See page 15.)

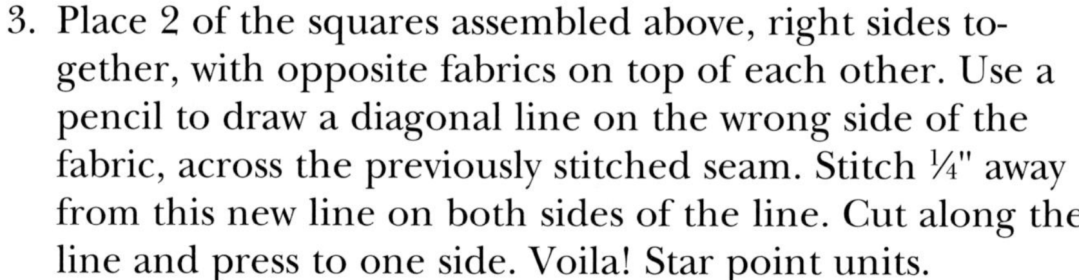

3. Place 2 of the squares assembled above, right sides together, with opposite fabrics on top of each other. Use a pencil to draw a diagonal line on the wrong side of the fabric, across the previously stitched seam. Stitch ¼" away from this new line on both sides of the line. Cut along the line and press to one side. Voila! Star point units.

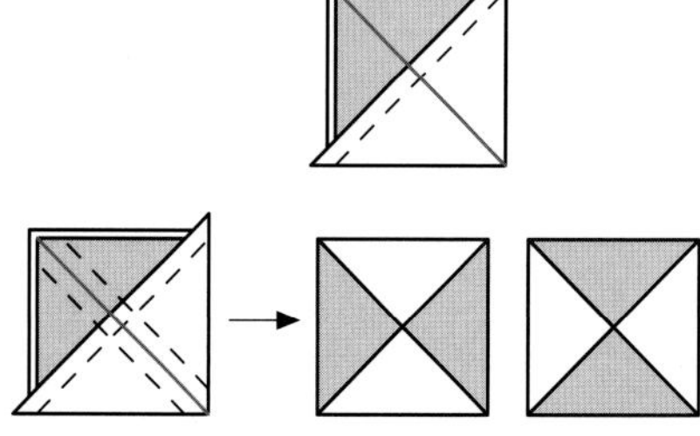

4. Cut 3"-wide strips from Fabric C; then crosscut the strips into 3" x 3" squares. See chart below.

	Number of Strips and Squares							
	Crib/Lap		*Twin*		*Dbl/Q*		*King*	
Fabric	**Strips**	**Squares**	**Strips**	**Squares**	**Strips**	**Squares**	**Strips**	**Squares**
C (star)	1	3	1	5	1	10	2	15

5. Assemble the blocks, following the piecing diagram at right to make the required number of Star blocks.

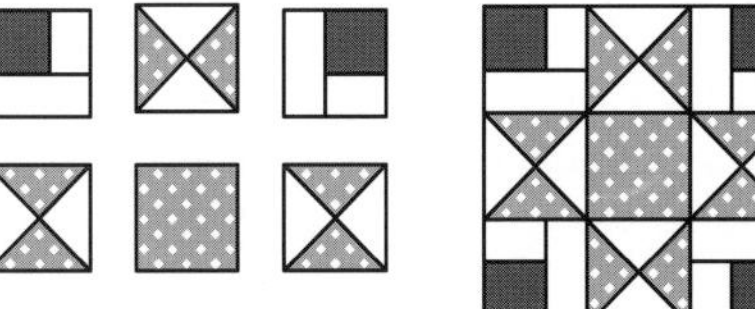

Star Block

Quilt Top Assembly and Finishing

1. Arrange blocks, following the quilt plan on page 24. Place Block A in all 4 corners; then alternate Blocks A and B to create the design. *Randomly* place Star blocks in the Block B position.
2. Sew the blocks together, using the "pairs of pairs of pairs" assembly method described on page 16 in the General Directions.
3. Cut the strips for each border and the binding. (See chart below.) Stitch the inner border strips together, end to end. Measure the quilt top for side borders and cut border strips to fit as described on page 17. Attach to the quilt with ¼"-wide seams, being careful not to stretch either the quilt or the borders. Repeat for the top and bottom borders. You can miter your border corners or simply overlap them. (See pages 17–19.) Always press the seams toward the border. Repeat for middle and outer borders.

		Number of Strips			
Fabric	***Strip Width***	***Crib/Lap***	***Twin***	***Dbl/Q***	***King***
Inner Border	2"	5	7	8	10
Middle Border	4½"	6	8	9	11
Outer Border	2"	6	8	10	11
Binding	3"	6	8	10	11

4. Quilt, using your favorite method. Quilt stars in the B blocks to match the Star blocks and quilt in-the-ditch on the Star blocks. Quilt the A blocks diagonally through the center of the block in both directions. There are stars in the middle border, too, because in Durango the skies are absolutely laced with stars!
5. Bind the edges of the quilt.

Quilting Diagrams

Block A

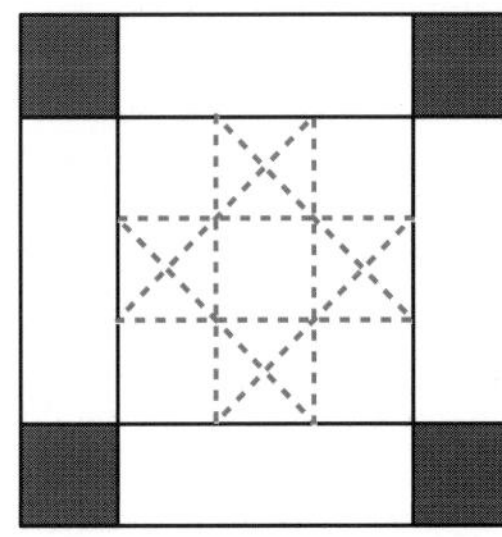

Block B

Star Block

Spinwheels

by Kim Gjere

Kim Gjere is a Colorado native, though from the other side of the mountains. She came here in 1978 as assistant controller for Ft. Lewis College, a position she held for two years. With a duo major, she thought she wanted to teach, so, after meeting and marrying her husband, Dick, she left the college and substituted for two years. Their family now includes Sara and Jeff.

Kim made her first quilt in 1979, then waited until '85 to make a second quilt. A founding member of the LaPlata Quilters Guild, she became thoroughly involved with quilting in 1986 and now teaches classes at Animas Quilts. "Puppy Parade" in Jackie's book *Tessellations* is one of Kim's quilts.

Spinwheels started as a Quarter Log Cabin, but spun out into this strip-set pinwheel quilt, reminiscent of the Durango and Silverton Narrow Gauge Railroad.

The Durango and Silverton Narrow Gauge Railroad delights visitors every year with its scenic trip between Durango and Silverton, fifty miles away. In the peak of the summer season, there are four trains each day, and residents can identify each engineer by the "tunes" he plays on the whistle.

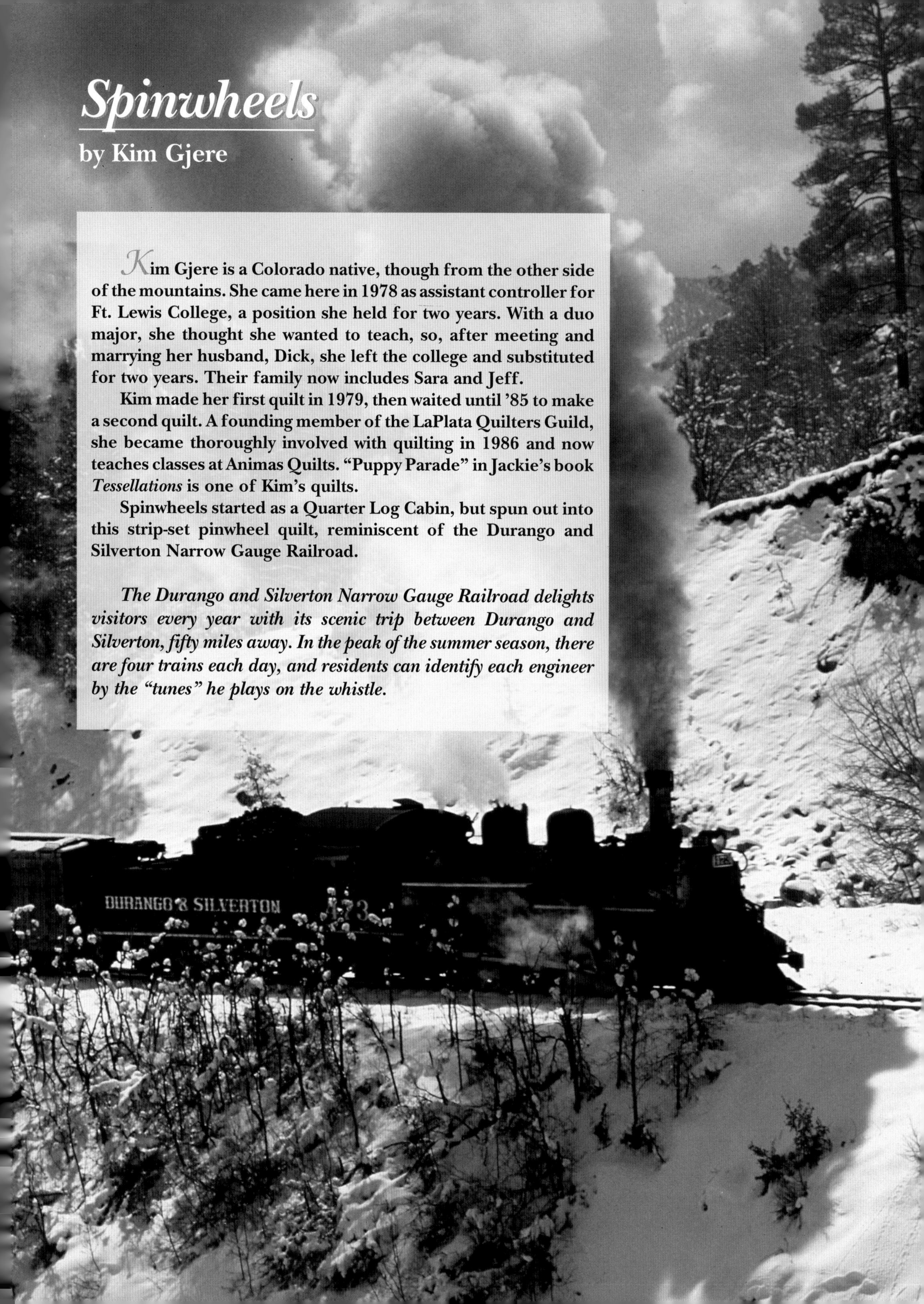

Spinwheels, by Kim Gjere, 1992, Durango, Colorado, 42" x 62". This easy-to-piece quilt is made from one block, which is strip pieced. I like the illusion that this quilt is not quite straight.

Beginner

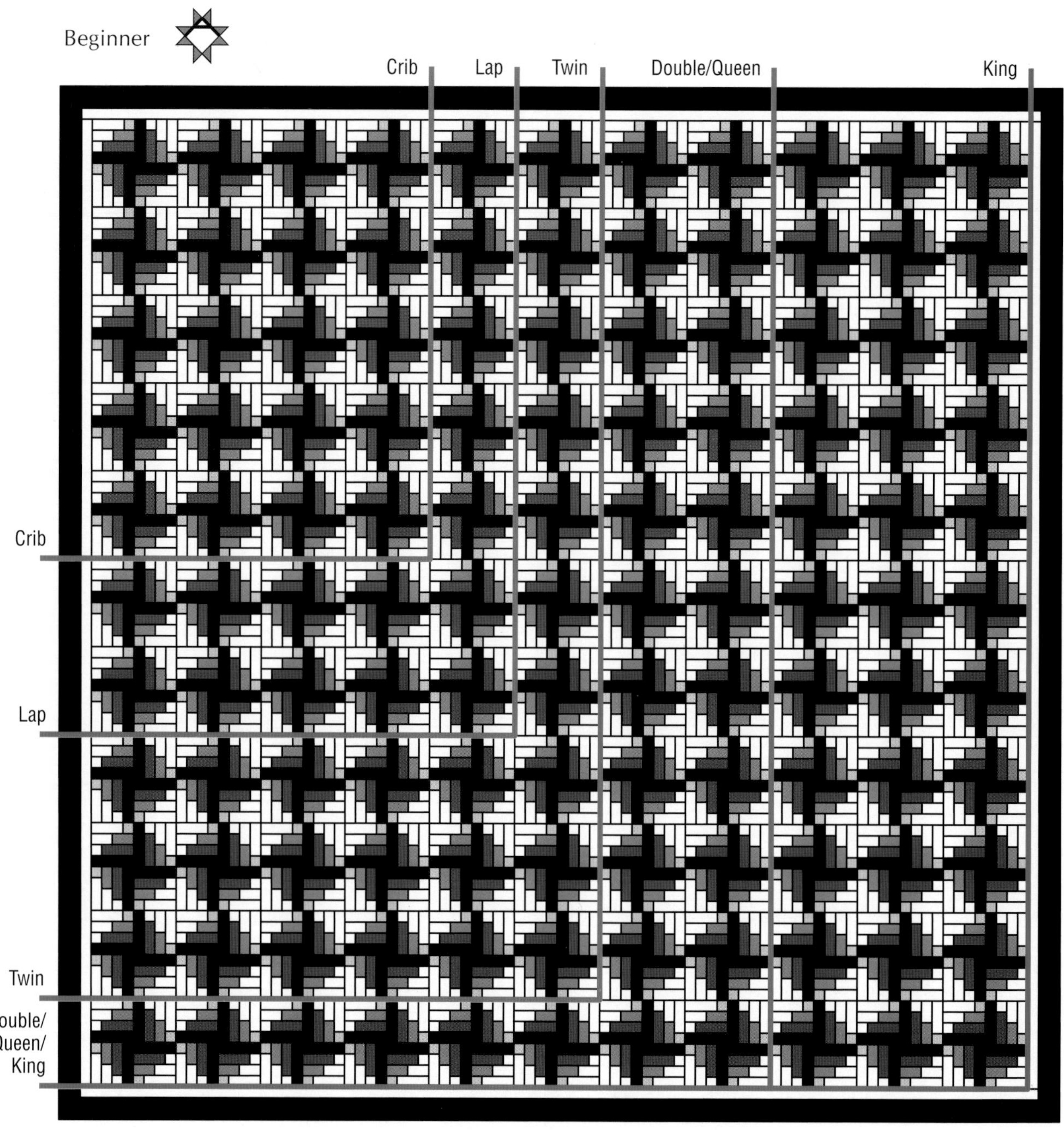

Quilt Plan

QUILT SIZES

Crib	*Lap*	*Twin*	*Dbl/Q*	*King*
Finished Size	**Finished Size**	**Finished Size**	**Finished Size**	**Finished Size**
38" x 46"	46" x 62"	62" x 94"	78" x 102"	102" x 102"
No. of Blocks	**No. of Blocks**	**No. of Blocks**	**No. of Blocks**	**No. of Blocks**
20	35	60	88	121
Block Layout	**Block Layout**	**Block Layout**	**Block Layout**	**Block Layout**
4 x 5	5 x 7	6 x 10	8 x 11	11 x 11

MATERIALS: 44"-wide fabric

Purchase the required yardage for the quilt size you are making. When selecting fabrics for the wheel, choose four values of one color: light, medium-light, medium, and dark. The "spin" works best if the dark is 1 1/2 to 2 steps darker than the medium.

Fabric Requirements in Yards

	Crib	*Lap*	*Twin*	*Dbl/Q*	*King*
Light	1/4	1/4	1/2	5/8	7/8
Medium-Light	1/4	1/2	3/4	1	1 3/8
Medium	1/3	5/8	1	1 1/2	2
Dark	1/2	3/4	1 1/4	1 7/8	2 1/2
Background*	7/8	1 3/8	2 1/2	3 3/8	4 5/8
Border 2	1/2	1/2	5/8	5/8	7/8
Border 3	—	—	1 1/8	1 1/4	1 3/8
Binding	1/2	5/8	3/4	7/8	1
Backing	1 1/2	2 7/8	5 5/8	6 1/8	9 1/8
Piecing for Backing					

*Includes yardage for Border 1.

CUTTING

Cut all strips across the width of the fabric (crosswise grain).

Fabric	*Strip Width*	Number of Strips *Crib*	*Lap*	*Twin*	*Dbl/Q*	*King*
Light	1 1/2"	3	5	9	13	18
Medium-Light	2 1/2"	3	5	9	13	18
Medium	3 1/2"	3	5	9	13	18
Dark	4 1/2"	3	5	9	13	18
Background	1 1/2"*	7	10	16	21	27
	2 1/2"	3	5	9	13	18
	3 1/2"	3	5	9	13	18
Border 2	2 1/2"	5	6	7	8	10
Border 3	4 1/2"	—	—	8	9	10
Binding	3"	5	6	8	9	10

*Includes strips for Border 1. Set extras aside for step 2, "Quilt Top Assembly and Finishing," page 35.

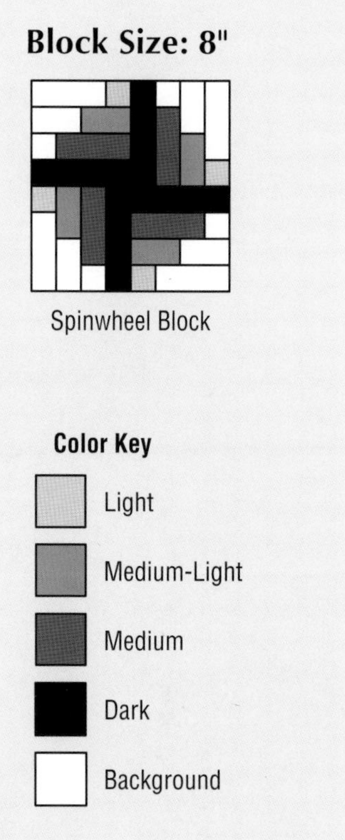

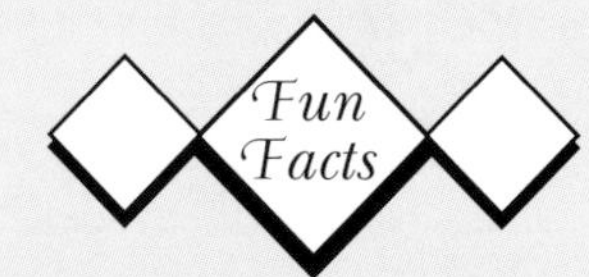

Will Rogers made a brief visit to Durango and quickly caught a glimpse of what it held . . . "then Wiley hit a beeline over the tops of the mountains to Durango, a beautiful little city, out of the way and glad of it, gold, silver and Mesa Verde Cliff Dwelling Ruins, . . ."

Directions

Blocks

Each block is made of up 4 rows. Row 1 is a segment of the 4½"-wide dark wheel strip.

1. Make 3 different strip sets for rows 2, 3, and 4 as shown in the piecing diagram below. Press the seams toward the wheel fabric. Crosscut the strips into 1½"-wide segments. See chart below for the number of strip sets and 1½"-wide segments required for the size you are making.

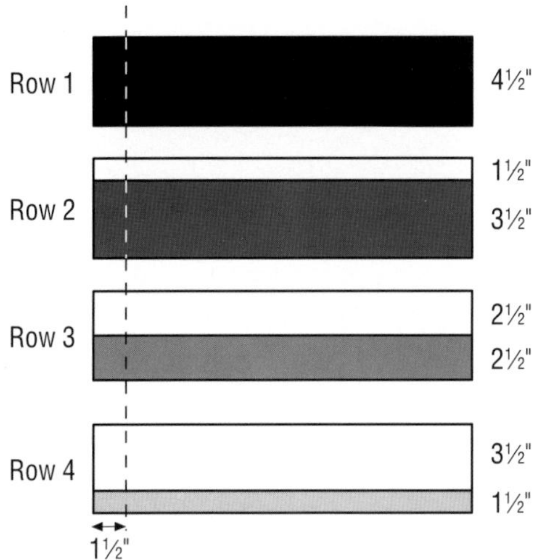

Number of Strips and Segments

	Crib		*Lap*		*Twin*		*Dbl/Q*		*King*	
	Strip Sets	**1½" Segments**	**Strip Sets**	**1½" Segments**	**Strip Sets**	**1½" Segments**	**Strip Sets**	**1½" Segments**	**Strip Sets**	**1½" Segments**
Row 1	3	80	5	140	9	240	13	352	18	484
Row 2	3	80	5	140	9	240	13	352	18	484
Row 3	3	80	5	140	9	240	13	352	18	484
Row 4	3	80	5	140	9	240	13	352	18	484

Layer your strip sets together to streamline crosscutting and sewing rows together. Lay row 1 right side up on the cutting board. Place row 2 wrong side up on top of row 1, with the wheel fabric toward the bottom. Now crosscut these 2 rows together. Repeat with rows 3 and 4.

2. You are now ready to sew the rows together. Follow the piecing diagram at right to make ¼ of a block. Press the seams in the direction of the arrows. This pressing plan allows seams to interlock when sewing the blocks together.

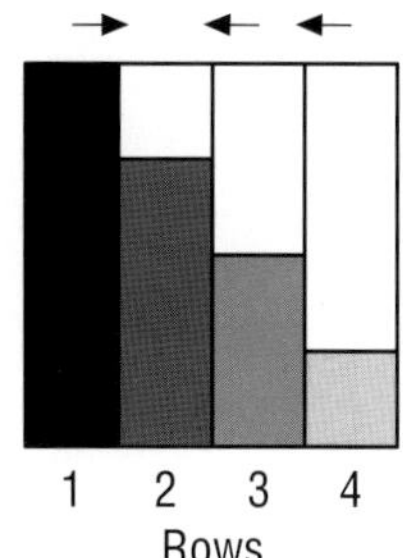

3. Sew 4 quarter blocks together to make the Pinwheel block as shown. Make the required number of blocks (page 32).

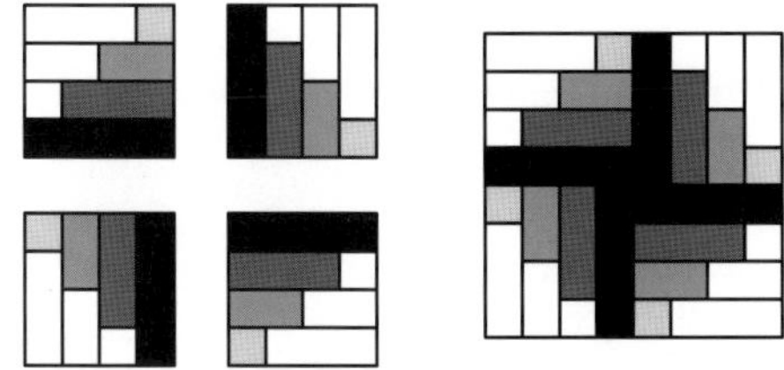

Quilt Top Assembly and Finishing

1. Arrange the completed blocks, following the quilt plan on page 32. Sew the blocks together, using the "pairs of pairs of pairs" assembly method described on page 16 in the General Directions.
2. Add borders next. All sizes have a 1" finished inner border, followed by a 2" finished border. The twin, double/queen, and king sizes have a 4" finished outer border. Cut border strips, following the cutting chart on page 33. Use the remaining 1½"-wide background strips for Border 1. Stitch the border strips together, end to end, and attach to the quilt with ¼"-wide seams. Measure quilt top for borders as shown on page 17. Being careful not to stretch either the quilt or the border, sew the borders to the sides, then to the top and bottom edges of the quilt. Always press the seams toward the border. Repeat for Border 2 and Border 3.
3. Quilt, using your favorite method. Use free-motion machine quilting to emphasize the "spin" of the wheels and stipple quilt in the background.
4. Bind the edges of the quilt.

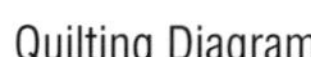

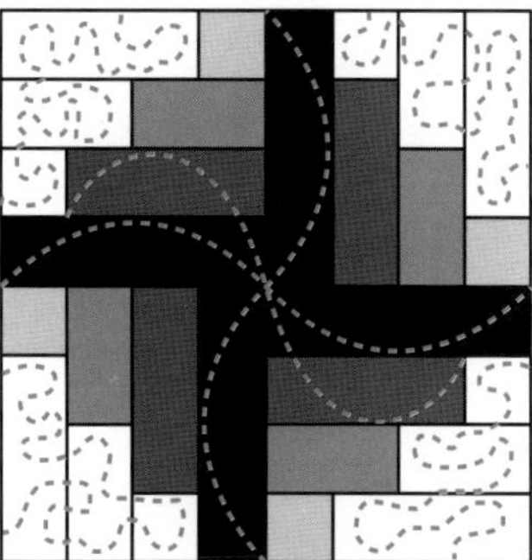

Sentimental Star

by Becky Smith

When selecting a college, Becky Smith , a Colorado native, chose Ft. Lewis in Durango, where she earned her B.A. in teacher education. After graduation, she decided to stay here and taught fifth grade for five years, before choosing semiretirement to raise her family. In 1990, she was wrangled into taking a class with friends at Animas Quilts, and like others before her, she became hooked!

Becky found the outdoor side of her nature in Durango. She spends a great deal of her free time skiing, hiking, hunting, and horseback riding. She is also sentimentally attached to Durango, where she met her husband, Rick, and where they enjoy family life with children Eileen and Tim. We all enjoy the tales she shares about her annual fall hunting trips with the men in her family. Becky says she "aims and misses deer and elk equally well."

With an abundance of wildlife, the fall hunting season attracts natives and visitors alike. One of Jackie's favorite sights was when she spotted a huge herd of majestic elk peacefully grazing in a field next to a "No Hunting Allowed" sign. She wondered when they learned to read so well!

	Block Size	Number of Blocks			
		Lap	*Twin*	*Dbl/Q*	*King*
Block A	7½" x 7½"	18	39	59	85
Block B	7½" x 7½"	17	38	58	84
Block C	4½" x 7½"	10	16	20	24
Block D	4½" x 7½"	14	18	24	28
Block E	4½" x 4½"	4	4	4	4

MATERIALS: 44"-wide fabric

Purchase the required yardage for the quilt size you are making.

Fabric Requirements in Yards

	Lap	*Twin*	*Dbl/Q*	*King*
Chain	1⅛	2¼	3¼	4½
Star	⅝	1⅛	1½	2⅛
Background and Inner Border	3¼	4⅔	6⅔	8⅞
Middle Border	¼	⅜	⅝	¾
Outer Border	⅜	⅝	1	1¼
Binding	⅔	¾	1	1⅛
Backing	3⅜	5⅞	6¾	10⅛
Piecing for Backing				

CUTTING

Cut all strips across the width of the fabric (crosswise grain).

Fabric	*Strip Width*	Number of Strips			
		Lap	*Twin*	*Dbl/Q*	*King*
Chain	2"	6	12	15	23
Star	2¾"	2	3	4	6
	2⅜"	3	6	8	12
Background	8"	8	8	12	16
	5"	3	4	5	6
	3½"	1	2	2	2
	2¾"	2	3	4	6
	2"	8	17	25	35
Inner Border	2"	5	9	14	19
Middle Border	1¼"	6	10	15	20
Outer Border	2"	6	10	15	20
Binding	3"	7	11	16	21

Blocks

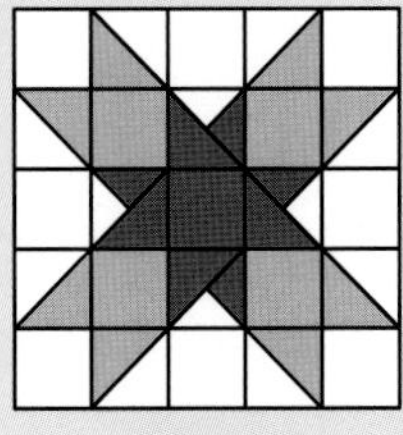

Block A

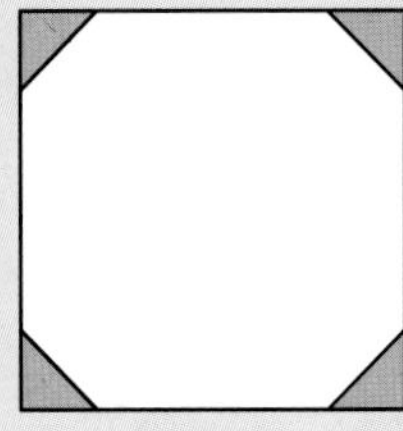

Block B

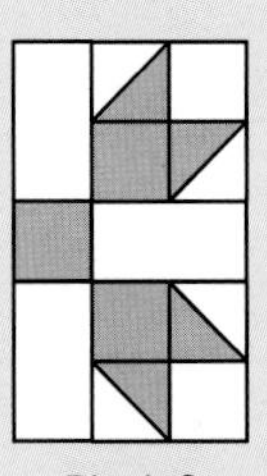

Block C

Block D

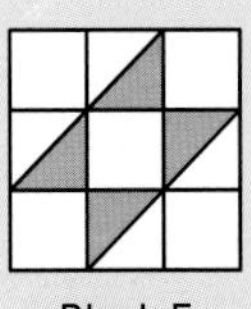

Block E

Directions

Block A

Choose one of the following methods to make half-square triangle units.

Preprinted Grid Paper

Grid paper is great for making half-square triangle units because it is a preprinted sheet with squares and diagonal stitching lines. It is accurate and easy! See page 14. To use grid paper for this quilt, cut the required number of 15" x 20" pieces from the chain and background fabrics as shown in the chart below.

		Number of Pieces			
Fabric	***Size***	***Lap***	***Twin***	***Dbl/Q***	***King***
Chain	15" x 20"	2	4	6	8
Background	15" x 20"	2	4	6	8

Strip Method

If grid paper is not available in your local quilt shop, use the strip method to make the required number of half-square triangle units.

1. Cut strips 2⅜" wide from the chain and background fabric; then crosscut the strips into 2⅜" squares. See chart below.

Number of Strips and Squares

	Lap		***Twin***		***Dbl/Q***		***King***	
Fabric	**Strips**	**Squares**	**Strips**	**Squares**	**Strips**	**Squares**	**Strips**	**Squares**
Chain	6	100	12	196	17	284	24	396
Background	6	100	12	196	17	284	24	396

2. Place a chain and background square together, with right sides facing, and mark a diagonal line from corner to corner on the wrong side of the lightest fabric. Sew an accurate ¼" on each side of the line. Don't sew on the line! Cut on the line and you'll have 2 half-square triangle units from each pair of squares. Press seams toward the darker fabric and trim the "dog-ear" corners.

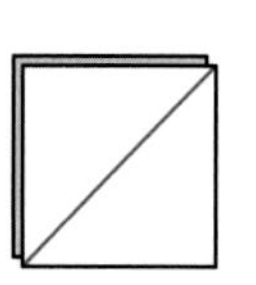

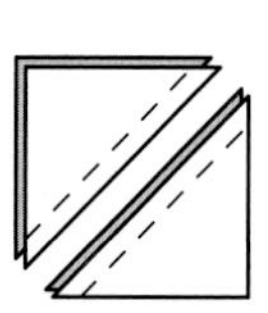

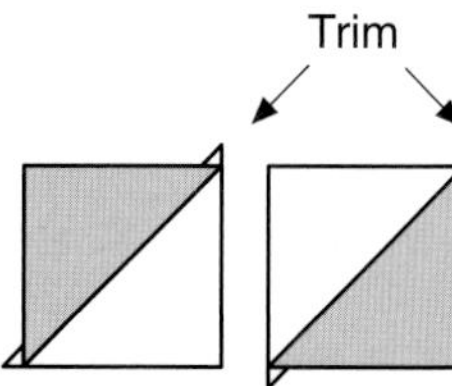

Super Star Points

1. Using the 2¾"-wide star strips and the 2¾"-wide background strips, crosscut the strips into 2¾" x 2¾" squares. Also crosscut the 2⅜"-wide star strips into 2⅜" x 2⅜" squares. See chart below.

		Number of Squares			
Fabric	***Size***	***Lap***	***Twin***	***Dbl/Q***	***King***
Star	2¾" x 2¾"	18	39	59	85
Background	2¾" x 2¾"	18	39	59	85
Star	2⅜" x 2⅜"	36	78	118	170

2. Place the 2¾" star squares and the 2¾" background squares together, with right sides facing. Mark a diagonal line from corner to corner on the wrong side of the background fabric. Sew ¼" on each side of the line. (Yes! This is just like the half-square triangle units made for Block A.) Cut on the line and press the seam to the dark side. Trim the "dog-ear" corners.
3. Mark a diagonal line from corner to corner on the wrong side of the 2⅜" star squares. Place the 2⅜" star square on top of the half-square triangle unit you just made in step 2 above, with the marked line on the 2⅜" square perpendicular to the seam of the half-square triangle unit. Stitch ¼" on each side of the line and cut apart on the line. Press the seams toward the big triangle. You did it!

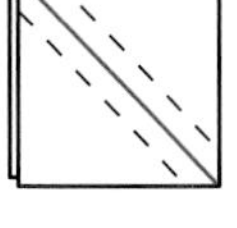

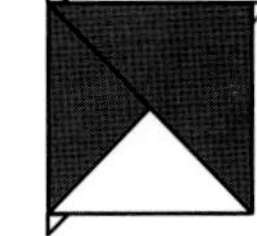

4. Using the 2"-wide chain strips and the 2"-wide background strips, crosscut the strips into 2" x 2" squares, to fill in the remainder of the A blocks.

		Number of Squares			
Fabric	***Size***	***Lap***	***Twin***	***Dbl/Q***	***King***
Chain	2" x 2"	90	195	295	425
Background	2" x 2"	136	304	464	672

5. Assemble Block A, following the piecing diagram at right. The 4 corners are identical, and if they are assembled and sewn to the centers as shown, you'll have a cleaner block. Make the required number of blocks. (See page 39.) You will not use all of the half-square triangles. Set the remainder aside for step 1 of Block C.

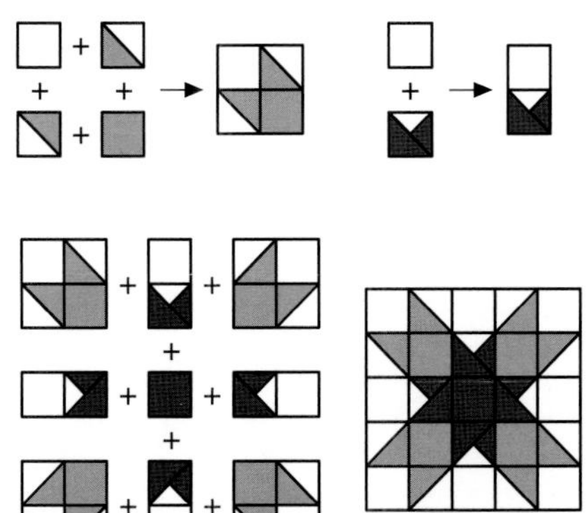

Block B

1. Crosscut the 2"-wide chain strips and the 8"-wide background strips into squares, following the chart below.

Fabric	Size	Number of Squares			
		Lap	Twin	Dbl/Q	King
Chain	2" x 2"	68	152	232	336
Background	8" x 8"	17	38	58	84

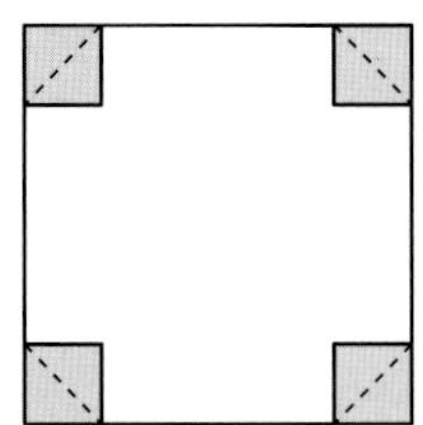

2. The 4 corners of the 8" squares will be covered with a "snowball" corner. Place a 2" chain square on top of the 8" background square, with right sides together, in each of the 4 corners. Stitch diagonally across the corners as shown.

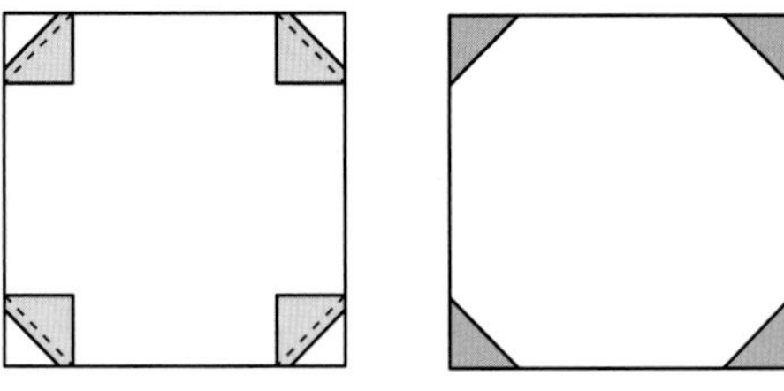

Block B

3. Trim the outer triangle section of the 2" chain square only ¼" from the stitching line, so you won't have to quilt through so many layers in the corners of the blocks. Do not trim the corners of the background square. (We call this cutting the baloney out of the sandwich.) Press the triangles toward the corners to show the right side of the chain fabric. Make the requitred number of blocks. (See page 39.)

Block C

Block C is the beginning of the border. It turns the "chain" back toward the quilt at the edges.

1. Crosscut the 2"-wide chain strips and 2"-wide background strips into 2" x 2" squares. Crosscut the 3½"-wide background strips into 2" x 3½" rectangles. Use the remainder of the half-square triangle units. See chart below.

Fabric	Size	Number of Segments and Units			
		Lap	Twin	Dbl/Q	King
Chain	2" x 2"	30	48	60	72
Background	2" x 2"	20	32	40	48
Background	2" x 3½"	30	48	60	72
Half-Square Triangle Units		40	64	80	96

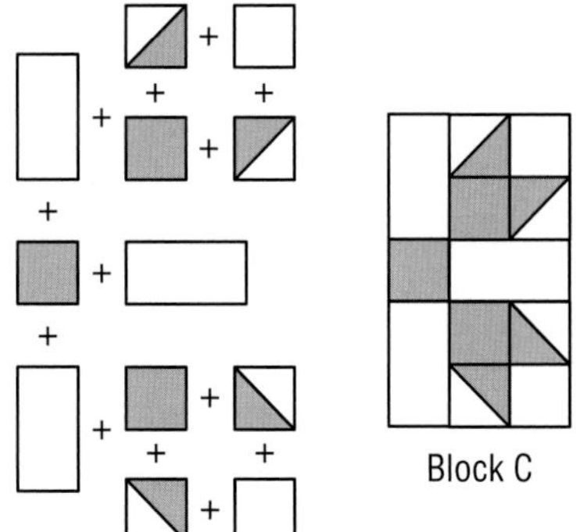

Block C

2. Assemble Block C, following the piecing diagram at left. Make the required number of blocks. (See page 39.)

Block D

1. Crosscut the 2"-wide chain strips into squares and the 8"-wide background strips into rectangles, following the chart below.

Fabric	Size	Number of Strips			
		Lap	***Twin***	***Dbl/Q***	***King***
Chain	2" x 2"	28	36	48	56
Background	5" x 8"	14	18	24	28

2. Stitch the 2" x 2" chain squares to 2 corners of the background rectangle as shown. Trim the outside corner of the chain square to within ¼" of the stitching line. Do not trim the corners of the background square. Press the triangles toward the corners. Make the required number of blocks. (See page 39.)

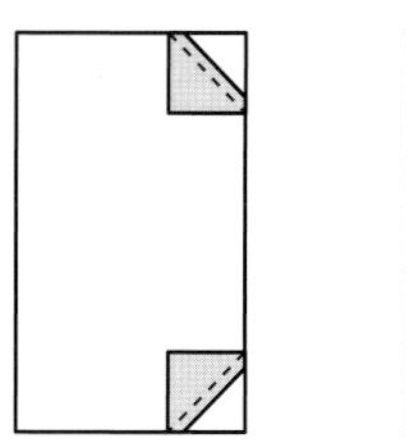

Block D

Block E (Corners)

These are made from the remaining half-square triangle units and 2" background squares. Make 4 blocks, following the piecing diagram at right.

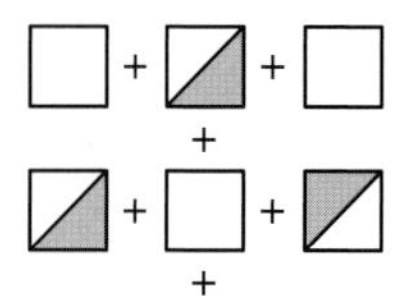
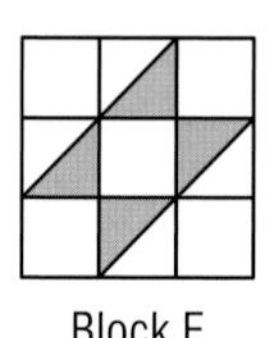
Block E

Quilt Top Assembly and Finishing

1. Arrange the blocks in the Sentimental Star design, following the quilt plan on page 38. Sew the blocks together, using the "pairs of pairs of pairs" assembly method described on page 16 in the General Directions.
2. Cut the required number of strips for each border as shown in the cutting chart on page 39. Sew the inner border strips together, end to end, and press the seams open. Measure the quilt top for borders as shown on page 17. Sew the inner border to the sides, then to the top and bottom edges of the quilt top. Repeat for the middle and outer borders.
3. Quilt, using your favorite method. Trace a favorite quilt stencil pattern onto Block B. Quilt in-the-ditch around the star points as shown below.

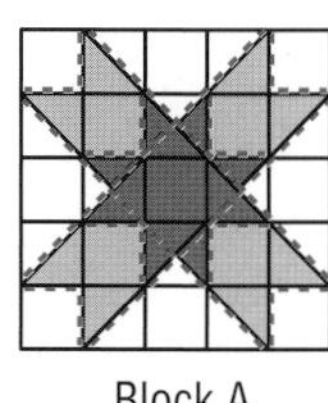
Block A

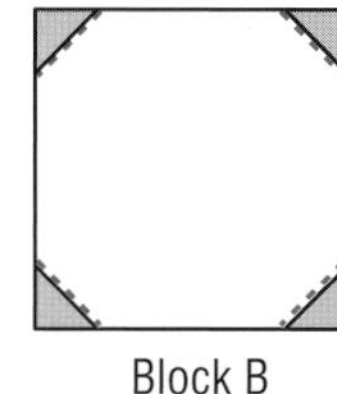
Block B
Design of choice in center

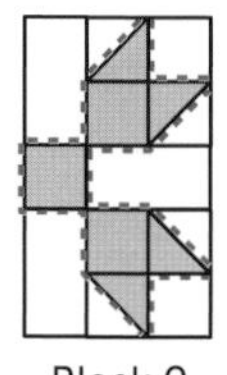
Block C

Block D

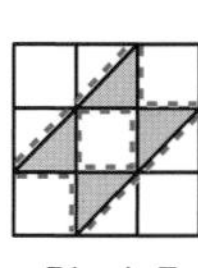
Block E

4. Bind the edges of the quilt.

Animas Crossing

by Melinda Malone

Melinda Malone moved to the Durango area in 1989 with her family. After the family settled in, she became interested in quilting and made friends quickly at Animas Quilts. Soon, employment became a necessity to support her new "habit," and Melinda began working one day a week at Animas Quilts. The mother of sons, Seth and Adam, Melinda has been designing quilts and teaching at Animas Quilts for three years.

Choosing the colors of the red cliffs just north of Durango and adding the trails made first by the wildlife, then by the ancient Native Americans, Melinda created this quilt, which is representative of the Hermosa Cliffs and the crossing of the Animas River.

You can enjoy the detail that the master builders we call the Anasazi (Navajo for Ancient Ones) accomplished centuries ago without the benefit of modern tools.

Animas Crossing, by Melinda Malone, 1992, Durango, Colorado, 57" x 57".

Advanced Beginner

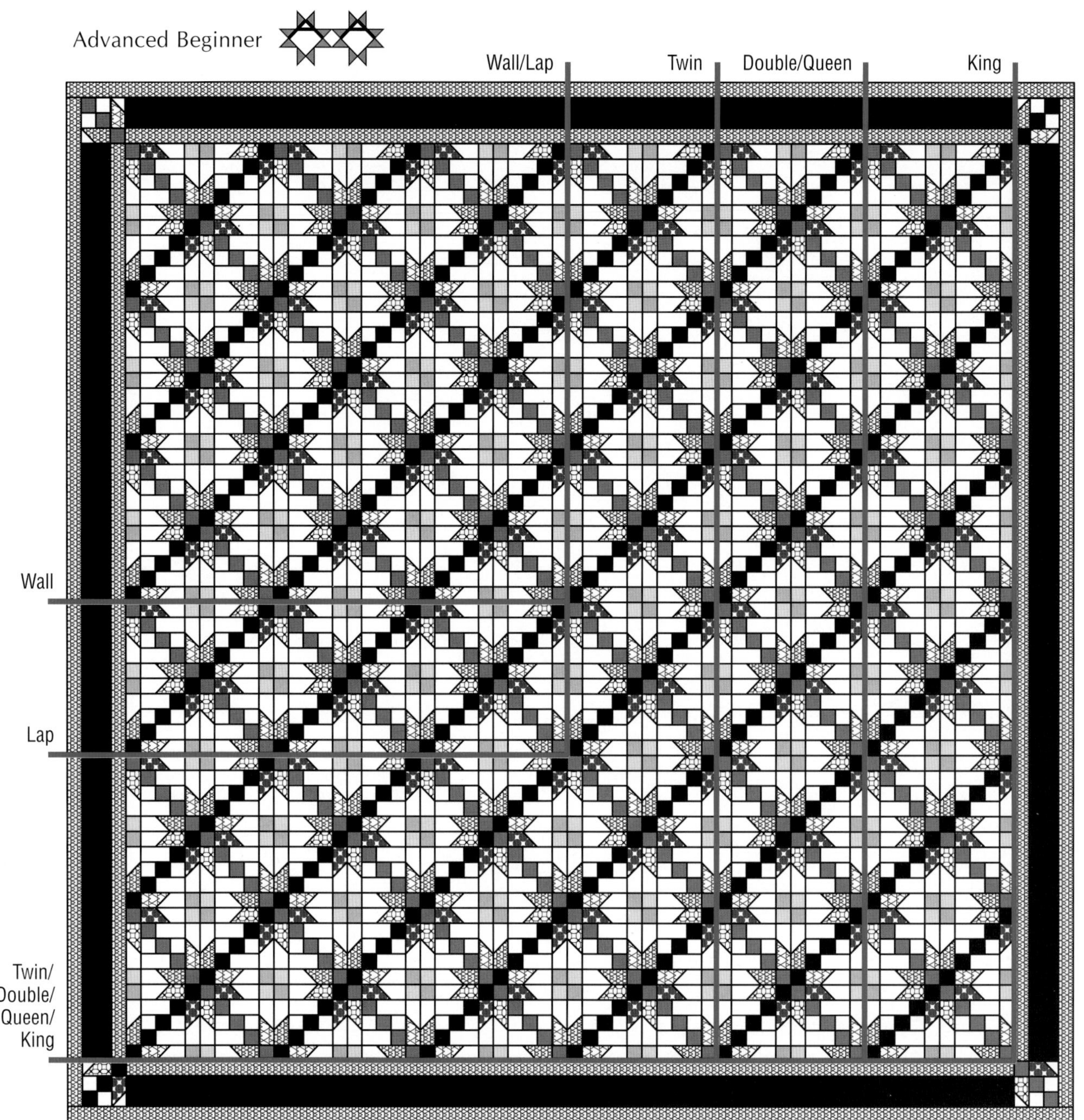

Quilt Plan

QUILT SIZES

Wall	*Lap*	*Twin*	*Dbl/Q*	*King*
Finished Size	**Finished Size**	**Finished Size**	**Finished Size**	**Finished Size**
57" x 57"	57" x 72"	72" x 102"	87" x 102"	102" x 102"
No. of Blocks	**No. of Blocks**	**No. of Blocks**	**No. of Blocks**	**No. of Blocks**
36	48	96	120	144
Block Layout	**Block Layout**	**Block Layout**	**Block Layout**	**Block Layout**
6 x 6	6 x 8	8 x 12	10 x 12	12 x 12

Number of Blocks

	Wall	Lap	Twin	Dbl/Q	King
Block A	18	24	48	60	72
Block B	18	24	48	60	72

Block Size: 8"

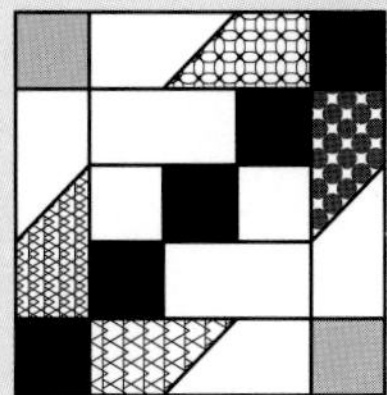
Block A

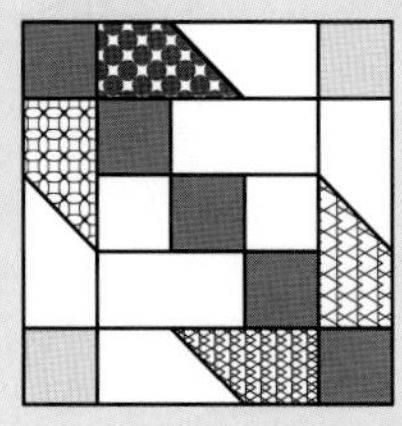
Block B

Color Key

- Star #1
- Star #2
- Star #3
- Star #4
- Chain #1
- Chain #2
- Corner #1
- Corner #2
- Background

MATERIALS: 44"-wide fabric

Purchase the required yardage for the quilt size you are making.

Fabric Requirements in Yards

	Wall	Lap	Twin	Dbl/Q	King
Star 1	1/4	1/4	1/2	5/8	3/4
Star 2	1/4	1/4	1/2	5/8	3/4
Star 3	1/4	1/4	1/2	5/8	3/4
Star 4	1/4	1/4	1/2	5/8	3/4
Chain 1	1/3	1/2	7/8	1	1 1/8
Chain 2	1/3	1/2	7/8	1	1 1/8
Corner 1	1/8	1/4	1/3	3/8	1/2
Corner 2	1/8	1/4	1/3	3/8	1/2
Background	1 1/2	2 1/8	3 3/4	4 1/2	5 3/8
Inner Border	1/3	3/8	1/2	1/2	5/8
Middle Border	5/8	2/3	7/8	7/8	1
Outer Border	3/8	1/2	5/8	5/8	5/8
Binding	5/8	2/3	7/8	1	1
Backing	3 1/2	3 1/2	6 1/8	7 7/8	9 1/8
Piecing for Backing					

CUTTING

Cut all strips across the width of the fabric (crosswise grain).

		Number of Strips				
Fabric	*Strip Width*	*Wall*	*Lap*	*Twin*	*Dbl/Q*	*King*
Background	2"	16	24	44	52	64
	3½"	4	6	10	12	14
Star 1	2"	3	4	8	10	12
Star 2	2"	3	4	8	10	12
Star 3	2"	3	4	8	10	12
Star 4	2"	3	4	8	10	12
Chain 1	2"	5	8	13	15	18
Chain 2	2"	5	8	13	15	18
Corner 1	2"	2	3	5	6	7
Corner 2	2"	2	3	5	6	7

Before you crosscut, set aside the following strips for strip sets.

		Number of Strips				
Fabric	*Strip Width*	*Wall*	*Lap*	*Twin*	*Dbl/Q*	*King*
Background	2"	4	8	12	12	16
	3½"	4	6	10	12	14
Chain 1	2"	3	5	8	9	11
Chain 2	2"	3	5	8	9	11

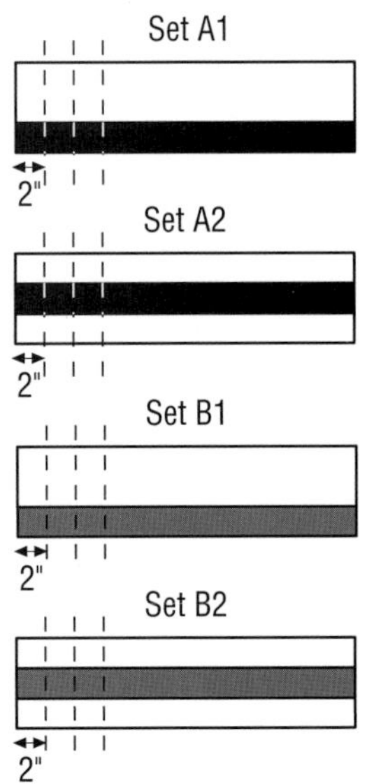

Directions

Quilt Blocks

The center section of both blocks is a Ninepatch unit made up of two different strip sets.

1. Make the strip sets shown in the diagram at left. Use antidirectional stitching as explained on page 12 in the General Directions and press the seams toward the chain fabric. Refer to the chart at the top of page 49 for the number of strips sets and 2"-wide segments required for the size quilt you are making.

Number of Strip Sets and Segments

	Wall		*Lap*		*Twin*		*Dbl/Q*		*King*	
	Strip Sets	**2" Segments**	**Strip Sets**	**2" Segments**	**Strip Sets**	**2" Segments**	**Strip Sets**	**2" Segments**	**Strip Sets**	**2" Segments**
A1	2	36	3	48	5	96	6	120	7	144
A2	1	18	2	24	3	48	3	60	4	72
B1	2	36	3	48	5	96	6	120	7	144
B2	1	18	2	24	3	48	3	60	4	72

2. Sew the 2"-wide segments together to make Ninepatch units as shown at right.
3. Make the diagonal star units that attach to all 4 sides of the Ninepatch units. Crosscut 2"-wide strips to make segments as shown in the chart below. Be accurate in cutting and counting, and it will be easy!

A1 + A2 + A1 (rev.) → Block A

B1 + B2 + B1 (rev.) → Block B

Number of Segments and Squares

	Size	*Wall*	*Lap*	*Twin*	*Dbl/Q*	*King*
Background	2" x 3½"	144	192	384	480	576
Star 1	2" x 3½"	36	48	96	120	144
Star 2	2" x 3½"	36	48	96	120	144
Star 3	2" x 3½"	36	48	96	120	144
Star 4	2" x 3½"	36	48	96	120	144
Chain 1	2" x 2"	36	48	96	120	144
Chain 2	2" x 2"	36	48	96	120	144
Corner 1	2" x 2"	36	48	96	120	144
Corner 2	2" x 2"	36	48	96	120	144

4. Using the 2" x 3½" segments of Star 1 and 3, and an equal number of 2" x 3½" background segments, assemble the first set of diagonal star units for Block A. Place a background rectangle on top of a star rectangle, with right sides together, positioned as shown at right.

   Stitch corner to corner, from an outside corner to the opposite outside corner. Trim excess fabrics to ¼" from the stitching line. Press seams toward the star fabrics. Repeat for all the Star 1 and Star 3 segments.

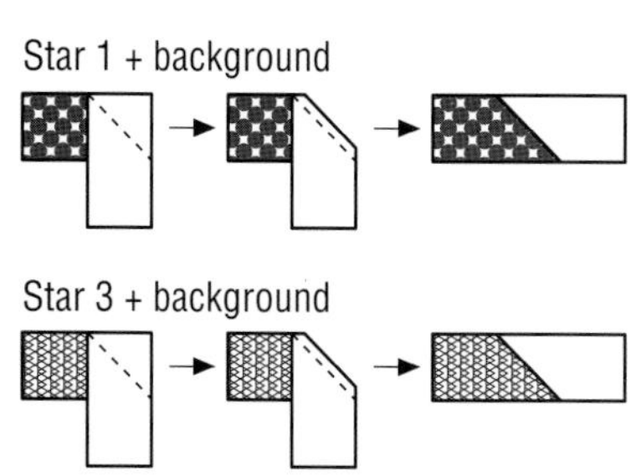

5. Using the 2" x 3½" segments of Star 2 and Star 4, and the remainder of the 2" x 3½" background segments, assemble a second set of diagonal star units for Block B. Place a background rectangle on top of a star rectangle, with right sides together, as shown at the top of page 50.

Note: These are mirror images of the previous sets made for Block A. The background rectangle is placed on the left-hand side of the star rectangle.

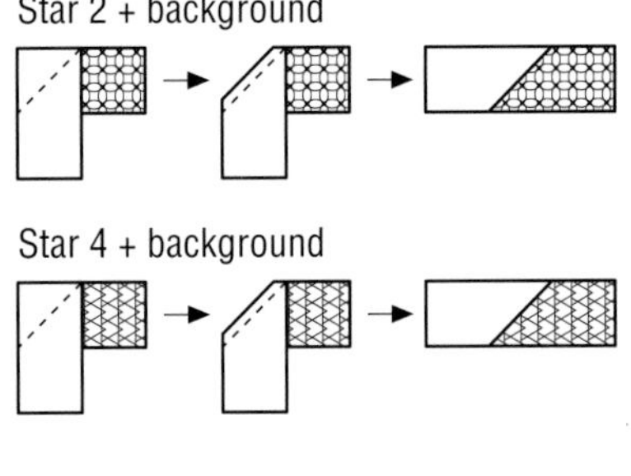

6. Stitch corner to corner, from an outside corner to the opposite outside corner. Trim excess fabric and press seams toward the star fabrics. Repeat for all the Star 2 and Star 4 segments.
7. Assemble Block A and Block B as shown in the piecing diagram below. Place star fabrics in the diagonal star units and 2" x 2" squares on specific sides of the Ninepatch units as shown below.

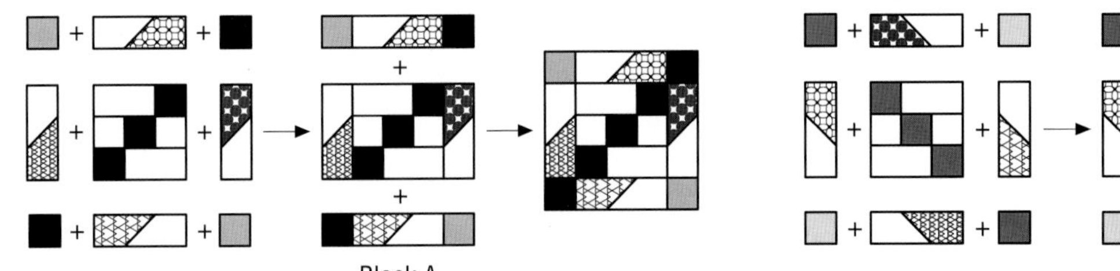

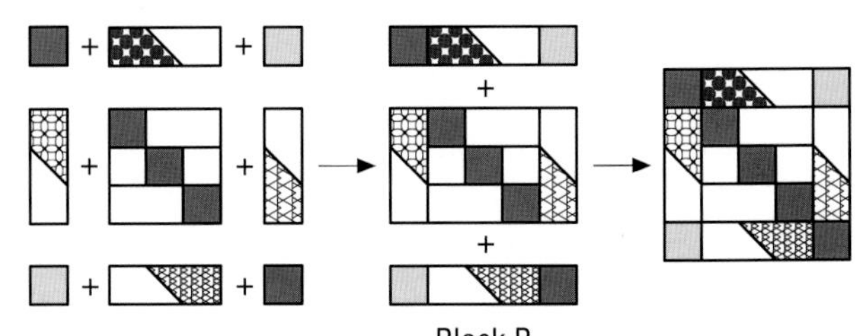

Quilt Top Assembly

Block A

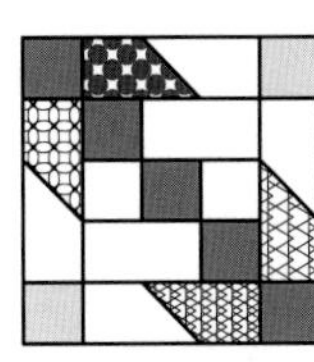
Block B

1. Arrange the blocks, alternating A and B blocks as described below and following the quilt plan on page 46.

   Begin the first row with Block B, then alternate the blocks, A/B/A/B/A, and so on. Begin the second row with Block A, then alternate B/A/B/A/B, and so on.

   Place Block A so the chain runs from the lower left to the upper right. Place Block B so the chain runs from the upper left to the lower right.

   Star fabrics 1 and 2 will always be in the upper part of the block rather than in the lower. Rotate your blocks, if necessary, to accomplish this.
2. Sew the blocks together, using the "pairs of pairs of pairs" assembly method described on page 16 in the General Directions. Press carefully.

Border Blocks

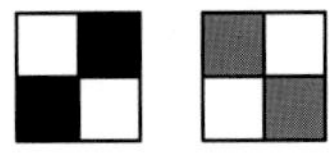

Make 4 border blocks for the corners from your "leftovers."

1. Make 2 Four Patch units, using 2" x 2" Chain 1 and 2" x 2" background squares; make 2 Four Patch units, using 2" x 2" Chain 2 and 2" x 2" background squares.

2. Make 8 diagonal star units, using 2 each of the 4 star fabrics. Place a 2" square of background on top of a 2" x 3½" star rectangle, right sides together, and stitch diagonally from corner to corner. The direction you stitch is very important. Star fabrics 1 and 3 are stitched in one direction, and star fabrics 2 and 4 are stitched in the opposite direction.

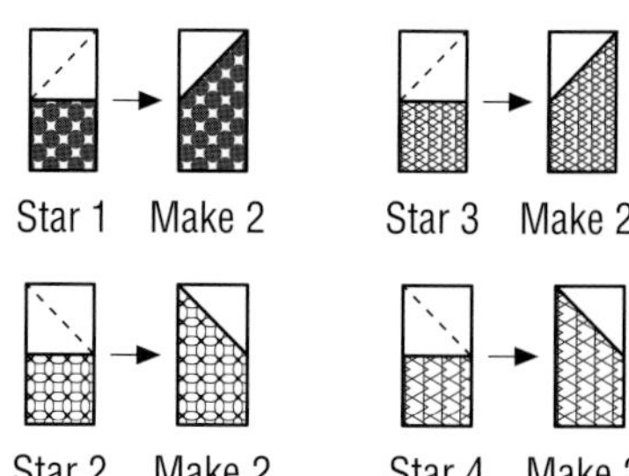

3. Cut 2 squares, each 2" x 2", from Chain 1, and 2 squares, each 2" x 2", from Chain 2.
4. Assemble the border blocks as shown in the piecing diagram at right.

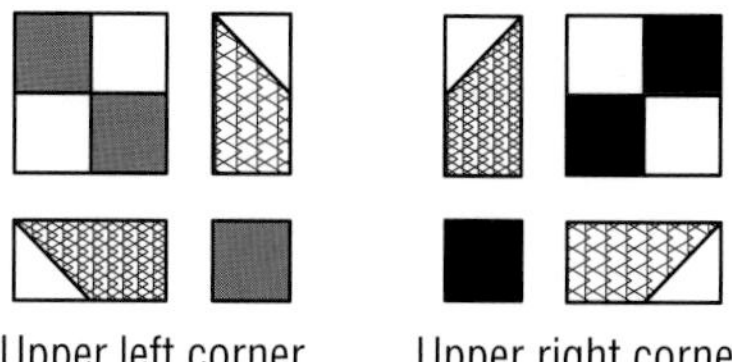
Upper left corner
Upper right corner

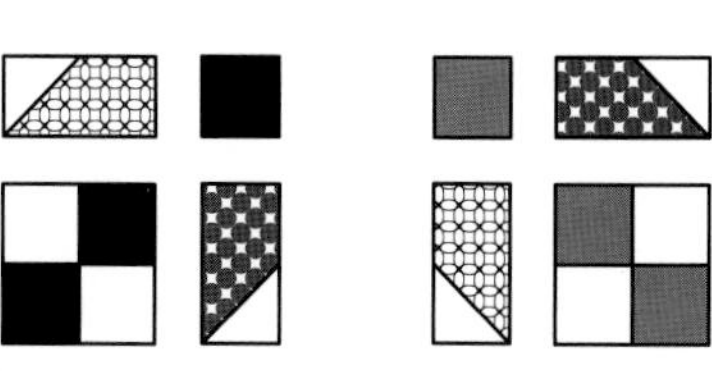
Lower left corner
Lower right corner

Quilt Finishing

1. Cut the required number of border strips and binding strips as shown in the chart below.

Fabric	*Strip Width*	**Number of Strips** *Wall*	*Lap*	*Twin*	*Dbl/Q*	*King*
Inner Border	2"	5	6	8	8	9
Middle Border	3½"	5	6	8	8	9
Outer Border	2"	6	7	9	10	10
Binding	3"	6	7	9	10	10

2. Sew the inner border strips together, end to end, to make one continuous strip. Press seams open. Repeat for the middle border; then sew the two borders together to make one pieced border unit.
3. Measure the length and width of the quilt top through the center, not at the outer edges. Cut 2 side borders to match the length and 2 borders for the top and bottom to match the width. Sew the 2 side borders to the quilt, with the star fabric (inner border) closest to the quilt. Sew the special border blocks to each end of the remaining 2 borders; then sew the borders to the top and bottom edges of the quilt top.

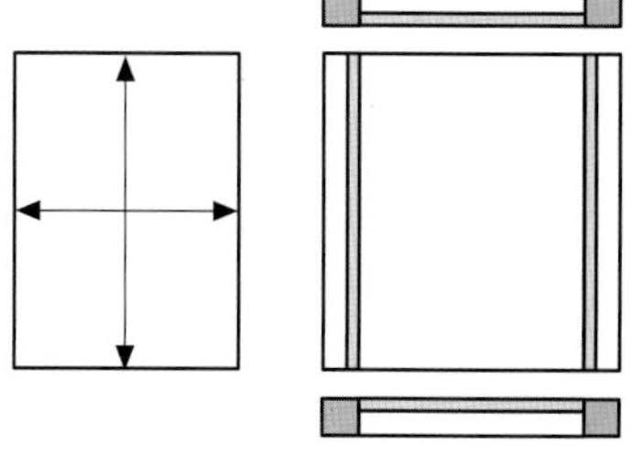

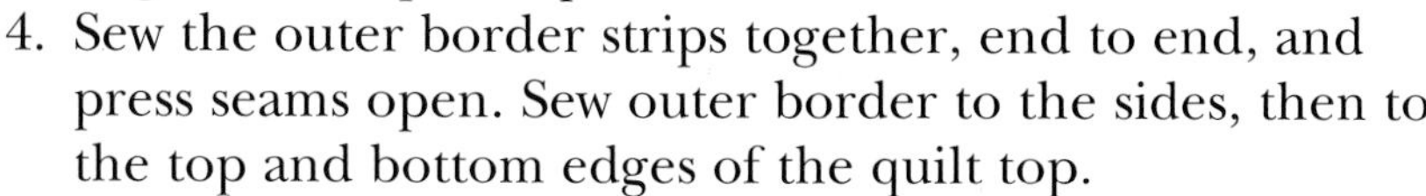

4. Sew the outer border strips together, end to end, and press seams open. Sew outer border to the sides, then to the top and bottom edges of the quilt top.
5. Quilt, using your favorite method. Quilt in-the-ditch and quilt a diamond shape where the corner blocks meet.
6. Bind the edges of the quilt.

Quilting Diagram
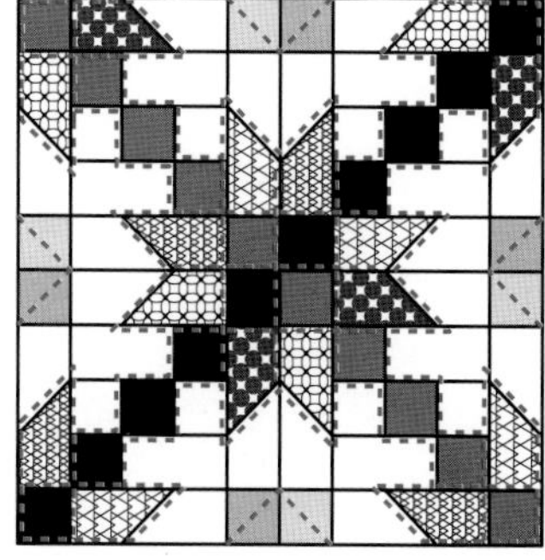

Star of the Southwest

by Suzanne Friend

I first met Suzanne Friend when she brought a cross-stitch project in for us to make into a quilt. A bit later, when she moved to town, we asked her to join our staff. Suzanne earned an art degree from DePauw University and then taught art at the elementary level. She and her husband, Joe, have raised two children, Lynn and Doug, now grown.

Suzanne's artistic talents are beautifully revealed in her quilts. The Star of the Southwest is a two-colored star with an "echo" that partially covers a blaze shooting above and below the star. Diamond-shaped "mountains" boldly cross other blazes and join the stars.

Suzanne's stars and blazes are medium values, in the colors of the rusty red cliffs that dominate our valley and the purplish red center of the blanket flower that grows in profusion here. The echo is a medium-light fabric from our Bou BouDima collection. (See page 7.) The background includes colors that suggest the range of purples and pinks we see in some of the wild flowers that grow here. Diamond-shaped mountains are medium dark in a bold bluish purple. The background fabric is light with muted colors that softly reflect the brighter colors of a Colorado sunset. Stipple quilting with silver thread makes the background sing.

Each January Durango has a special celebration called Snowdown. The festivities include hot air balloons, silly ski races, snow sculpturing, and lots of nonsense.

Star of the Southwest, by Suzanne Friend, 1992, Durango, Colorado, 68" x 88".

Intermediate

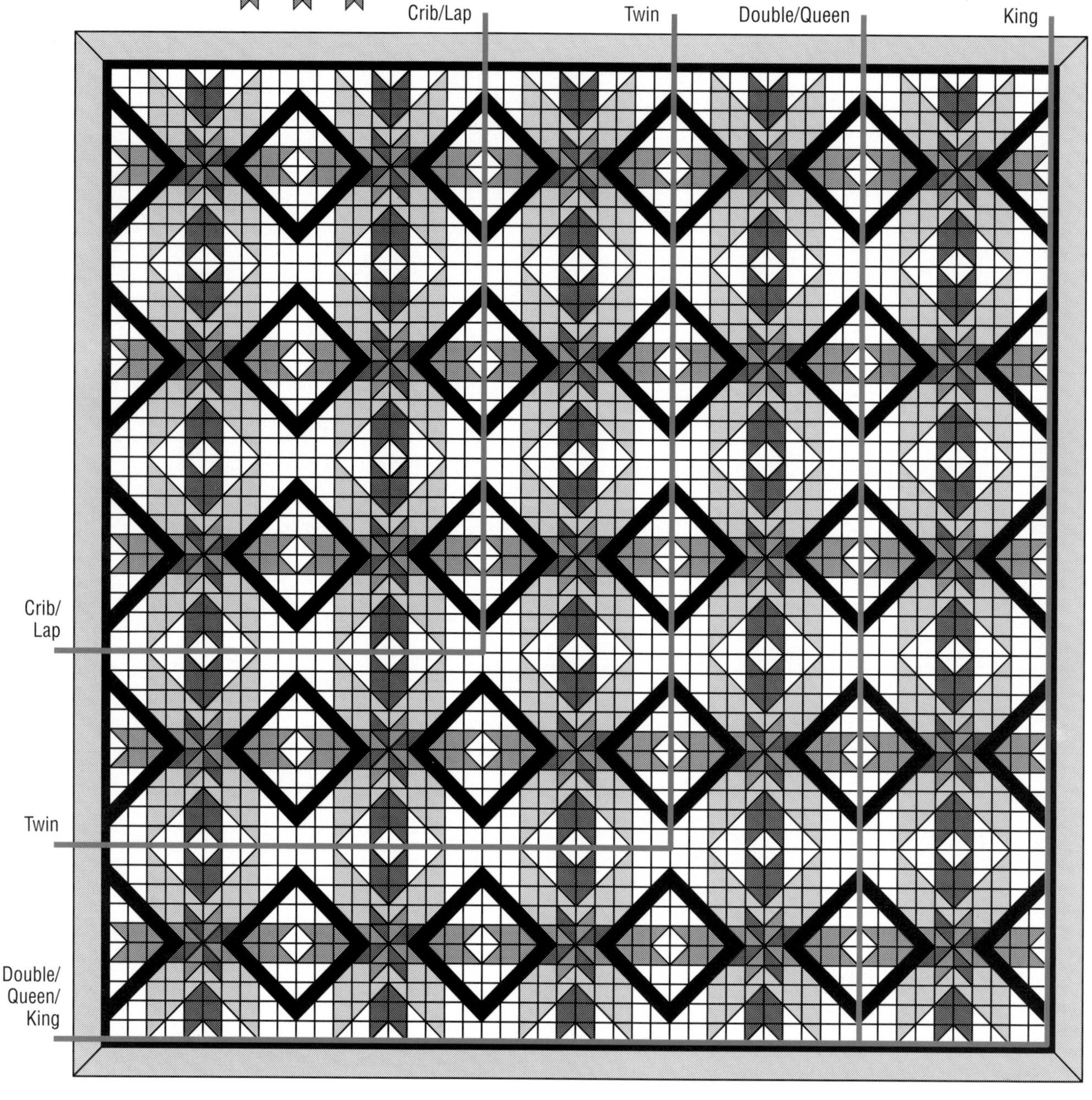

Crib/Lap Twin Double/Queen King

Crib/Lap

Twin

Double/Queen/King

Quilt Plan

QUILT SIZES

Crib/Lap	*Twin*	*Dbl/Q*	*King*
Finished Size 48" x 68"	**Finished Size** 68" x 88"	**Finished Size** 88" x 108"	**Finished Size** 108" x 108"
No. of Blocks 6	**No. of Blocks** 12	**No. of Blocks** 20	**No. of Blocks** 25
Block Layout 2 x 3	**Block Layout** 3 x 4	**Block Layout** 4 x 5	**Block Layout** 5 x 5

Number of Units

	Crib/Lap	Twin	Dbl/Q	King
Unit A (10")	12	24	40	50
Unit B (10")	12	24	40	50

MATERIALS: 44"-wide fabric

Purchase the required yardage for the quilt size you are making.

Fabric Requirements in Yards

	Crib/Lap	*Twin*	*Dbl/Q*	*King*
Star Blaze (medium #1)	5/8	1 1/4	1 1/2	1 7/8
Star Blaze (medium #2)	5/8	1 1/4	1 1/2	1 7/8
Echo (medium light)	7/8	1 3/4	2 7/8	3 1/2
Diamond (medium dark)	5/8	1 1/8	1 3/4	2 1/4
Background (light)	1 1/4	2 3/8	4	5
Inner Border	1/4	1/3	3/8	1/2
Outer Border	3/4	1	1 1/4	1 1/3
Binding	5/8	3/4	1	1
Backing	3	5 1/3	7 7/8	9 5/8
Piecing for Backing				

Block Size: 20"

Star Block
Each block is made up of four 10" units, 2 of Unit A and 2 of Unit B.

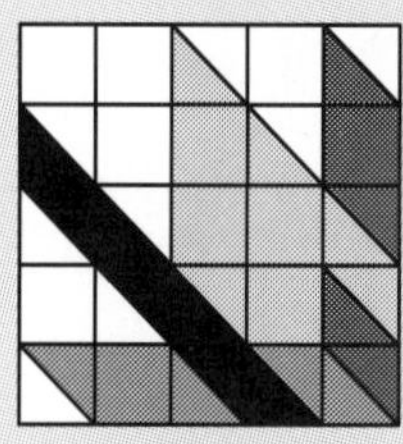

Unit A

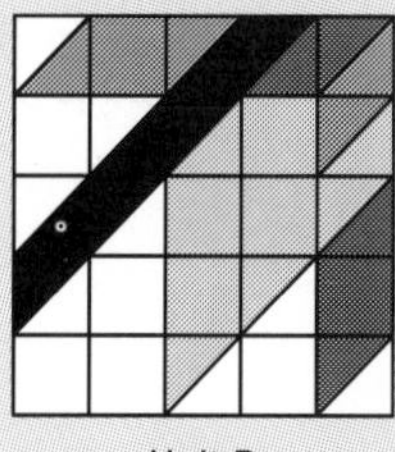

Unit B

Color Key

Directions

Blocks

These blocks are made up entirely of half-square triangle units and plain squares of fabric.

1. Make the required number of half-square triangle units. Use 2" preprinted grid paper, or draw your own 2⅞" grid on the wrong side of the lightest fabric from each combination. Refer to the instructions for half-square triangle units in the General Directions on pages 12–15.

   The following chart indicates the total number of 2⅞" squares needed of each fabric in each combination, to make the required number of half-square triangle units. As you make these units, mark the combination to make block assembly easy later on.

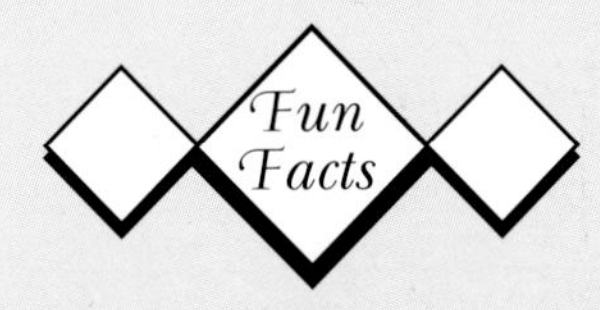

Munchies for Quiltmaking

M & M's®
(melt in your mouth, not on your quilt)

Popcorn
(unbuttered!)

Chocolate Orange Sticks
(the Orange part makes them healthy)

Peppermint Candies
(your quilt appreciates your fresh breath)

Pretzels
(bite size won't crumble)

Number of 2⅞" Squares

Fabric Combinations	*Crib/Lap*	*Twin*	*Dbl/Q*	*King*
Star #1	12	24	40	50
Star #2	12	24	40	50
Star #1	18	36	60	75
Echo	18	36	60	75
Star #2	6	12	20	25
Echo	6	12	20	25
Star #1	6	12	20	25
Diamond	6	12	20	25
Star #2	18	36	60	75
Diamond	18	36	60	75
Star #1	12	24	40	50
Background	12	24	40	50
Star #2	12	24	40	50
Background	12	24	40	50
Echo	24	48	80	100
Background	24	48	80	100
Diamond	48	96	160	200
Background	48	96	160	200
Diamond	12	24	40	50
Echo	12	24	40	50

2. For the plain squares, cut 2½"-wide strips of fabric; then crosscut the strips into 2½" x 2½" squares. One 2½" strip of 42"-wide fabric will yield 16 squares. If your fabric is less than 42" wide, you will need to cut an additional strip to cut the total number of squares required.

Number of Strips and Squares

	Crib/Lap		*Twin*		*Dbl/Q*		*King*	
	Strips	**Squares**	**Strips**	**Squares**	**Strips**	**Squares**	**Strips**	**Squares**
Star 1	2	24	3	48	5	80	7	100
Star 2	2	24	3	48	5	80	7	100
Echo	6	96	12	192	20	320	25	400
Background	8	120	15	240	25	400	32	500

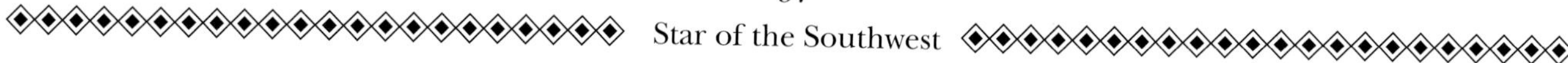

3. Assemble Unit A and Unit B, following the piecing diagram at right. Press the seams of alternate rows in opposite directions.

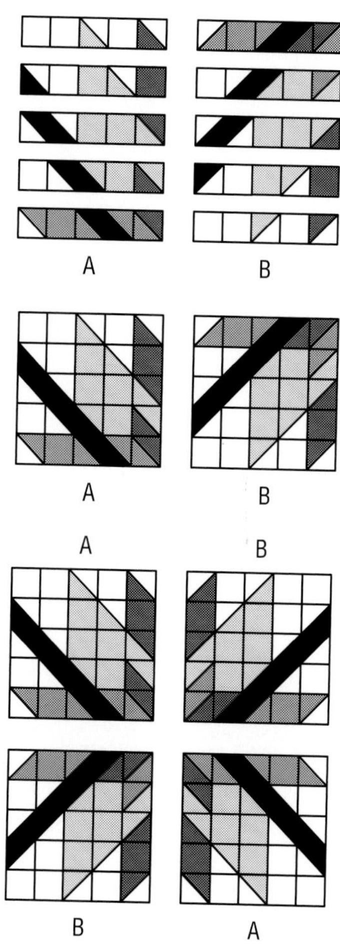

4. Join the rows in Unit A, making sure that seams and points match. Do the same for Unit B.

5. Sew 2 of Unit A and 2 of Unit B together to make a 20" block as shown at right. Make the required number of blocks as shown on page 55.

Quilt Top Assembly and Finishing

1. Arrange the blocks as shown in the quilt plan on page 54.
2. Cut strips for the borders and the binding as shown in the chart below.

Fabric	Strip Width	Number of Strips: Crib/Lap	Twin	Dbl/Q	King
Inner Border	1¼"	6	8	10	11
Outer Border	4"	6	8	10	11
Binding	3"	6	8	10	11

3. Stitch the inner border strips together, end to end, and press seams open. Measure quilt top for borders as shown on page 17. Sew inner border to the sides and then to the top and bottom edges of the quilt top. Repeat for the outer border. You may miter your borders or use borders with straight-cut corners.(See pages 17–19.) Always press the seams toward the outer edges.
4. Quilt, using your favorite method. Quilt in-the-ditch of the stars and the blazes shooting from them, the Bou BouDima "echoes," and the purple mountains that join to form diamonds. Stipple quilt the background.
5. Bind the edges of the quilt.

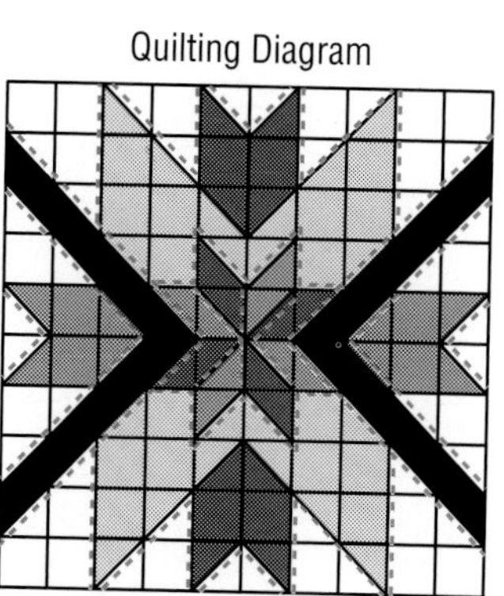

Heart's Desire

by Barbara Morgan

The only native Durangoan on our staff, Barbara Morgan is also a graduate of Ft. Lewis College. She taught kindergarten and physical education before becoming a nearly full-time mom. Our first employee at Animas Quilts, Barb teaches as well as operates our commercial quilting machine. Her quilt "Variable Reel" is featured in Jackie's book *Tessellations.*

Barb's home, which she shares with her husband, Rob, and their daughters, Crystal and Caitlin, is on the family ranch on the mesa south of town. From her home, she can see the beautiful mountains where she likes to hike. Barbara's quilt integrates the color of the western skies with the land where her heart is.

The blue columbine, Colorado's state flower, grows abundantly in the alpine meadows and in natural gardens. The gardener may select columbines in lots of hybrid colorings, but the periwinkle of the native plant speaks softly to hikers of the mountain trails.

Heart's Desire, by Barbara Morgan, 1992, Durango, Colorado, 52½" x 60".

Intermediate 

Double/Queen: **Finished Size:** 82½" x 105" **Block Size:** 3¾"

Quilt Plan

Lap Quilt: **Finished Size:** 52½" x 60" **Block Size:** 3¾" Quilt Plan

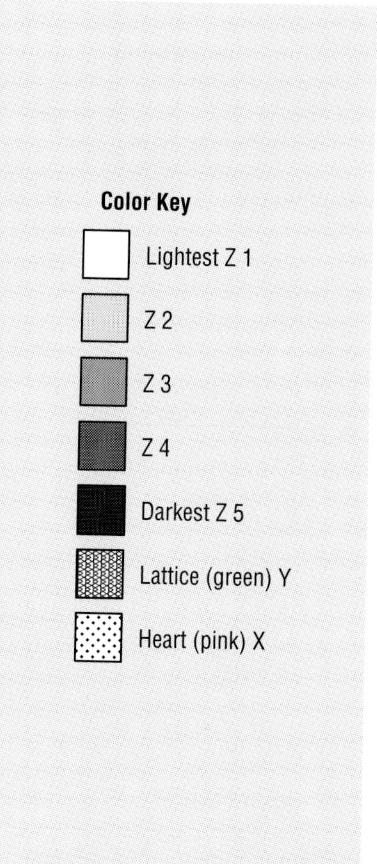

MATERIALS: 44"-wide fabric

Purchase the required yardage for the quilt size you are making.

Fabric Requirements in Yards

	Lap	*Dbl/Q*
Lightest Z 1	5/8	7/8
Z 2	1	1 5/8
Z 3	1	2 1/4
Z 4	7/8	3 1/3
Darkest Z 5	1/2	1 5/8
Lattice (green) Y	1/2	1 1/8
Heart (pink) X	1	1 7/8
Binding	1/2	7/8
Backing	3 1/4	6 1/4
Piecing for Backing		

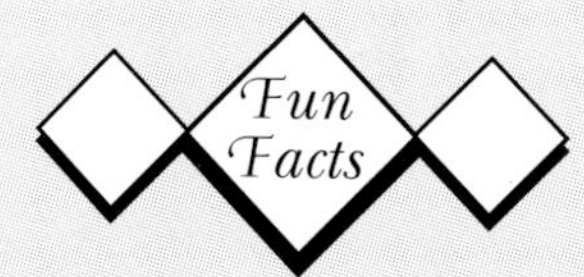

Set up your machine in front of the TV-VCR, put in a favorite movie, and sew! Generally you'll want a movie that doesn't make you follow too closely, so pick your old favorites, where you already know the story line.

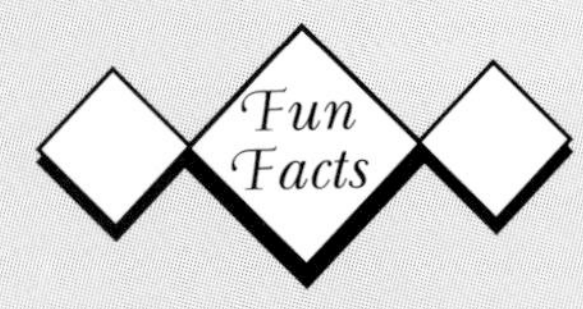

Parts of many movies have been filmed near Durango:

"Around the World in 80 Days" filmed the train scene with a D & RG locomotive, Shirley MacLaine, David Niven, Cantinflas, and Buster Keaton.

"Across the Wide Missouri" with Clark Gable

"Night Passage" with Jimmy Stewart

"Ticket to Tomahawk" with Anne Baxter and Marilyn Monroe

"Butch Cassidy and the Sundance Kid" with Robert Redford and Paul Newman

"City Slickers" with Billy Crystal, Daniel Stern, and Bruno Kirby

CUTTING

Cut all strips across the width of the fabric (crosswise grain).

		Number of Strips					
		Lap			***Dbl/Q***		
Fabric		***Strip Width***			***Strip Width***		
		1¾"	3"	4¼"	1¾"	3"	4¼"
Lightest	Z 1	4	1	2	5	2	3
	Z 2	6	2	3	8	3	7
	Z 3	4	2	4	8	6	9
	Z 4	4	1	4	12	5	15
Darkest	Z 5	3	1	2	6	4	6
Lattice (green)	Y	8	—	—	20	—	—
Heart (pink)	X	8	6	—	14	11	—

Directions

Please don't let the number of different strip sets overwhelm you. You probably make this many for any quilt but they are all the same. Look at this as a great deal of fun—and enjoy!

Pieced Blocks

Each of the 17 different blocks for this quilt is made of 3 strip sets or 2 strip sets and a plain 4¼"-wide strip. Remember to use antidirectional stitching (page 12) when sewing strip sets together. Always press the seams toward the heart fabric or the lattice fabric, so the seams will interlock when joining the blocks together.

1. Make strip sets, following the diagrams on pages 63 and 64. The X, Y, and Z labels at the left side of each strip set indicate the fabric placement. Below the strip set number, you will find the number of strip sets to make for the size quilt you are making, followed by the number of 1¾" segments to cut from the set(s). Label each strip set as you make it to avoid confusion.

Set 1 (Z-1, X, Z-1; 1¾")
Lap-1 set; cut 20 segments
Dbl-1 set; cut 24 segments

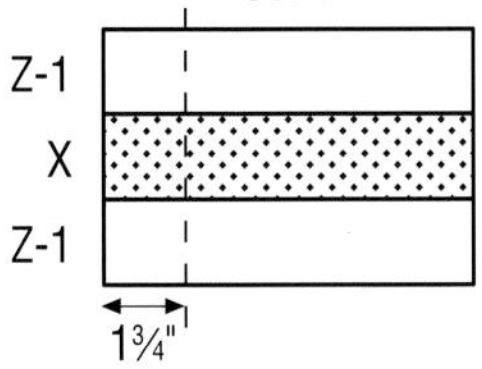

Set 2 (Z-2, X, Z-2; 1¾")
Lap-1 set; cut 8 segments
Dbl-1 set; cut 24 segments

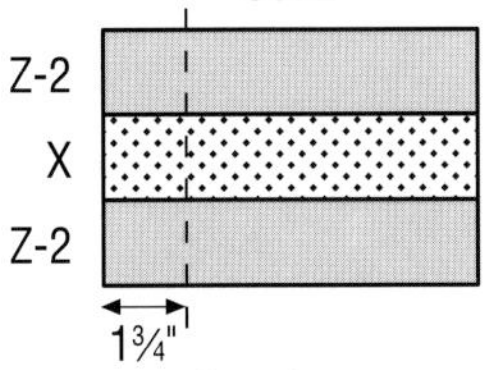

Set 3 (Z-3, X, Z-3; 1¾")
Lap-1 set; cut 8 segments
Dbl-1 set; cut 16 segments

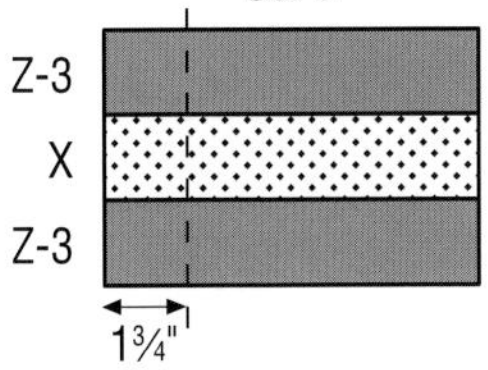

Set 4 (Z-4, X, Z-4; 1¾")
Lap-1 set; cut 8 segments
Dbl-2 sets; cut 28 segments

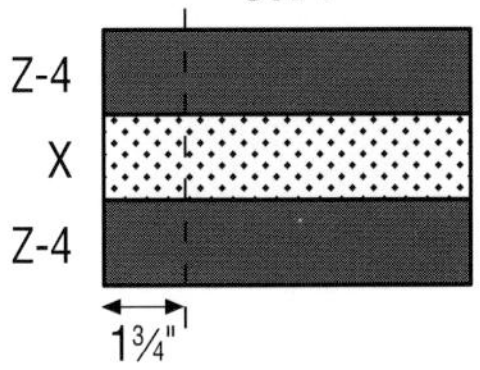

Set 5 (Z-5, X, Z-5; 1¾")
Lap-1 set; cut 16 segments
Dbl-1 set; cut 8 segments

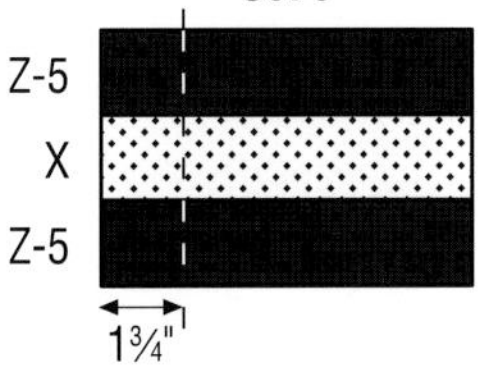

Set 6 (X, Z-1; 1¾")
Lap-1 set; cut 20 segments
Dbl-2 sets; cut 32 segments

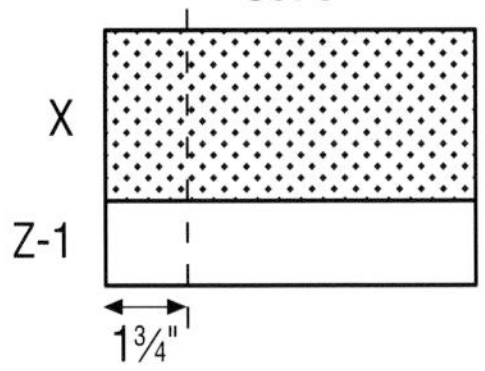

Set 7 (X, Z-2; 1¾")
Lap-1 set; cut 16 segments
Dbl-2 sets; cut 32 segments

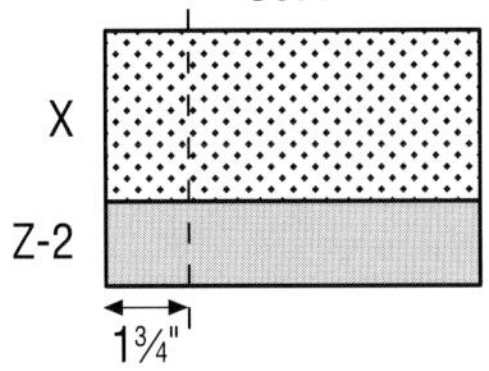

Set 8 (X, Z-3; 1¾")
Lap-2 sets; cut 32 segments
Dbl-3 sets; cut 68 segments

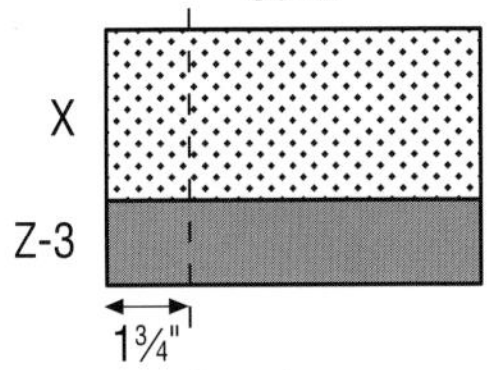

Set 9 (X, Z-4; 1¾")
Lap-1 set; cut 8 segments
Dbl-2 sets; cut 32 segments

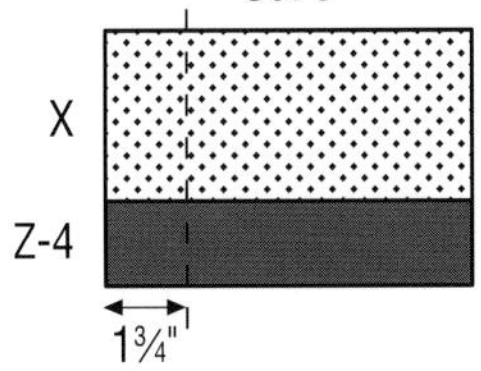

Set 10 (X, Z-5; 1¾")
Lap-1 set; cut 24 segments
Dbl-2 sets; cut 48 segments

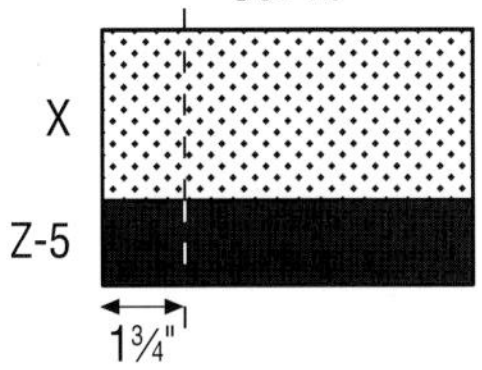

Set 11 (Y, Z-1; 1¾")
Lap-1 set; cut 16 segments
Dbl-1 set; cut 16 segments

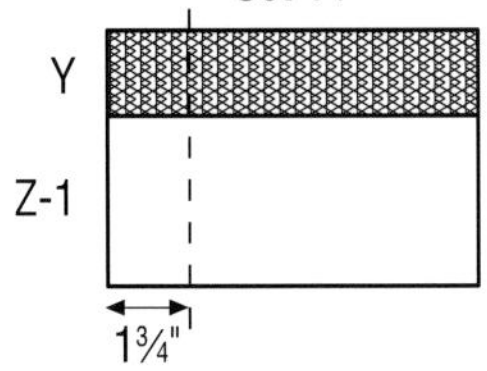

Set 12 (Y, Z-2; 1¾")
Lap-2 sets; cut 28 segments
Dbl-2 sets; cut 48 segments

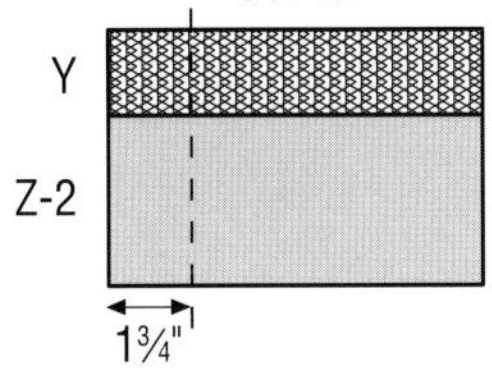

Set 13 (Y, Z-3; 1¾")
Lap-1 set; cut 20 segments
Dbl-3 sets; cut 52 segments

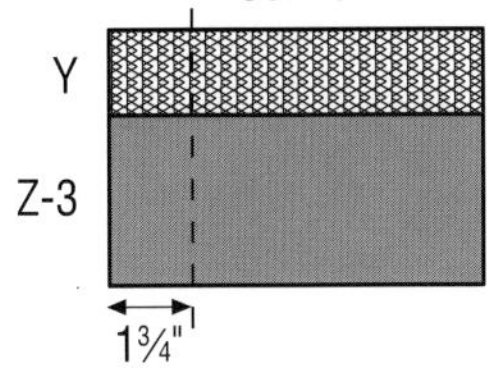

Set 14 (Y, Z-4; 1¾")
Lap-1 set; cut 20 segments
Dbl-4 sets; cut 88 segments

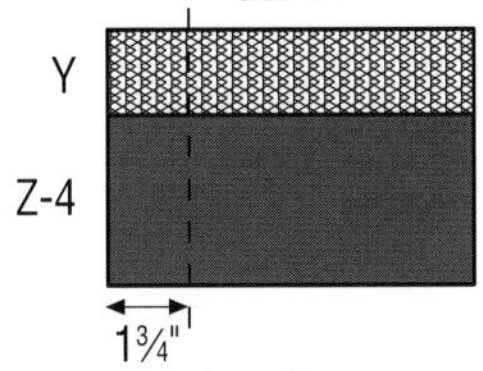

Set 15 (Z-2, Y, Z-1; 1¾")
Lap-1 set; cut 12 segments
Dbl-1 set; cut 12 segments

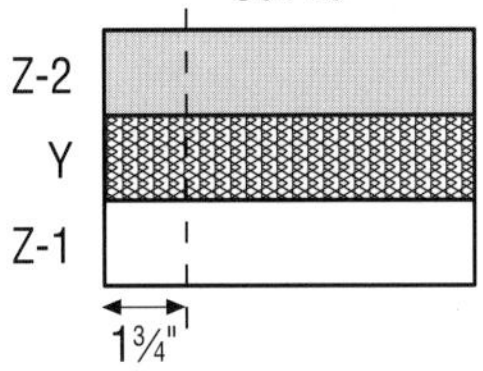

Set 16 (Z-2, Y, Z-2; 1¾")
Lap-1 set; cut 8 segments
Dbl-1 set; cut 8 segments

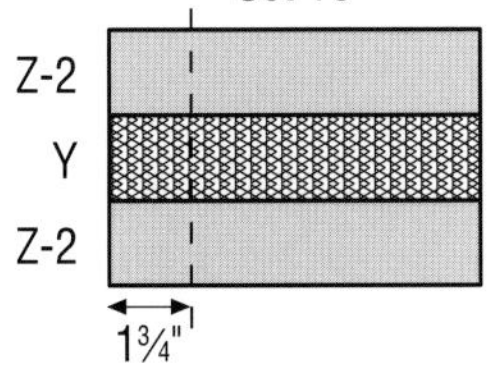

Set 17 (Z-4, Y, Z-3; 1¾")
Lap-1 set; cut 20 segments
Dbl-2 sets; cut 32 segments

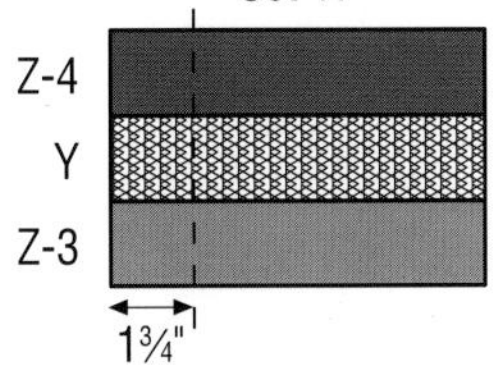

Set 18 (X, Z-2; 1¾")
Lap-1 set; cut 8 segments
Dbl-1 set; cut 8 segments

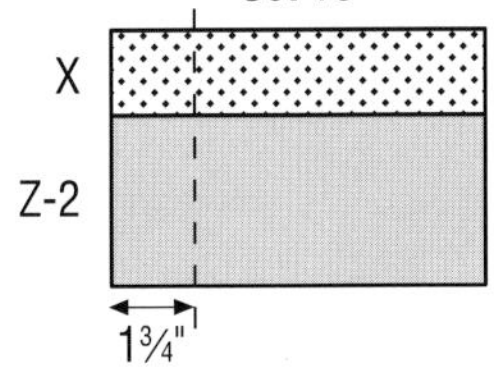

Set 19 (X, Z-3; 1¾")
Lap-1 set; cut 24 segments
Dbl-3 sets; cut 52 segments

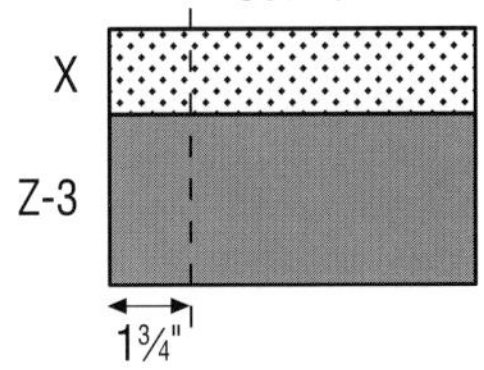

Set 20 (X, Z-5; 1¾")
Lap-1 set; cut 8 segments
Dbl-2 sets; cut 40 segments

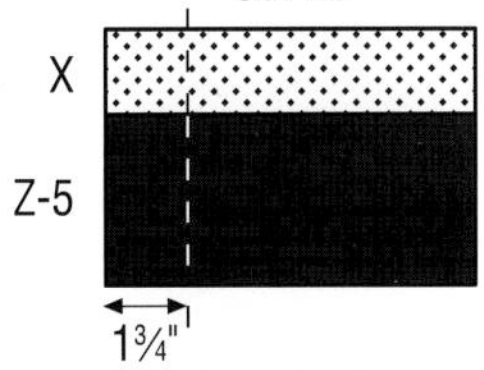

Note: Strip sets 21–25 are actually single strips of 4¼"-wide fabric and do not require any seaming. You will not use the full length of the 4¼"-wide strips. Set the remainder aside for the plain blocks.

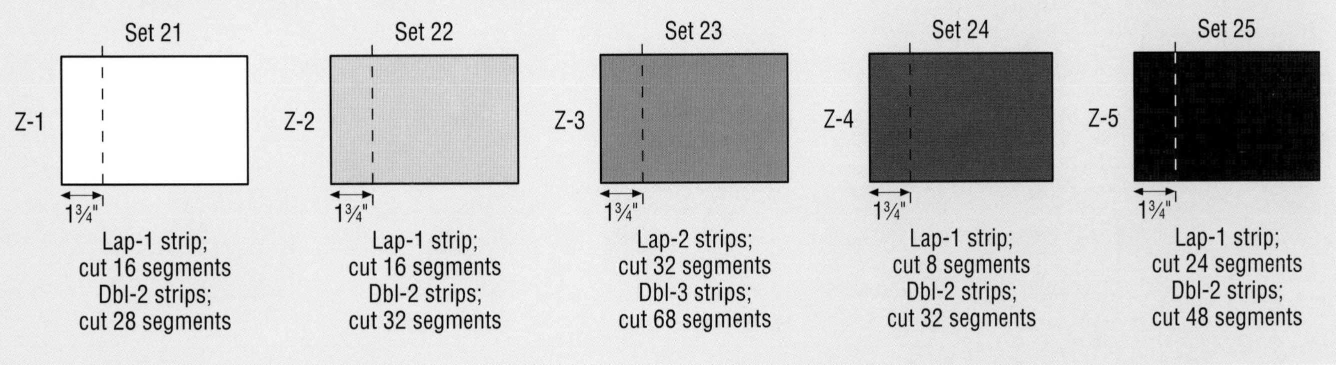

Note: Strip sets 26–31 are only required if you are making the Dbl/Q-size quilt.

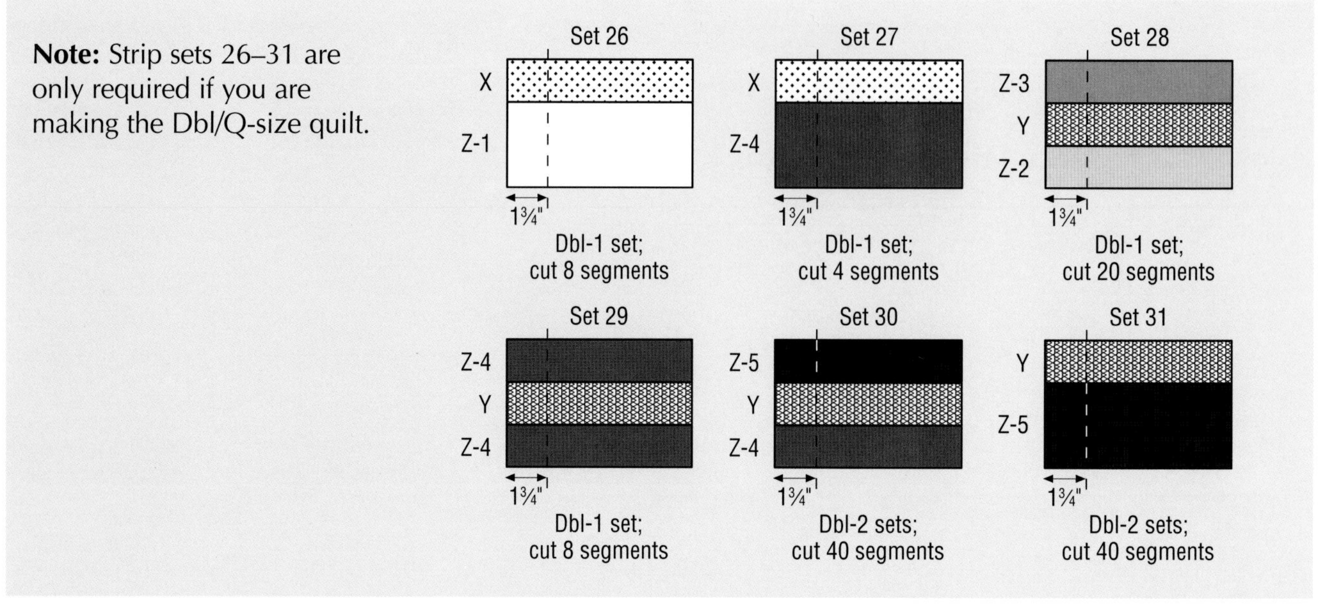

2. Crosscut the strip sets into the required number of 1¾"-wide segments.
3. Assemble the 1¾"-wide segments as shown in the piecing diagram below. The number above each row corresponds to the strip set from which the segment was cut. The number of each block needed for the Lap- or Dbl/Q-size quilt is given below the block. Make Blocks A–L for the Lap size, and Blocks A–Q for the Dbl/Q-size.

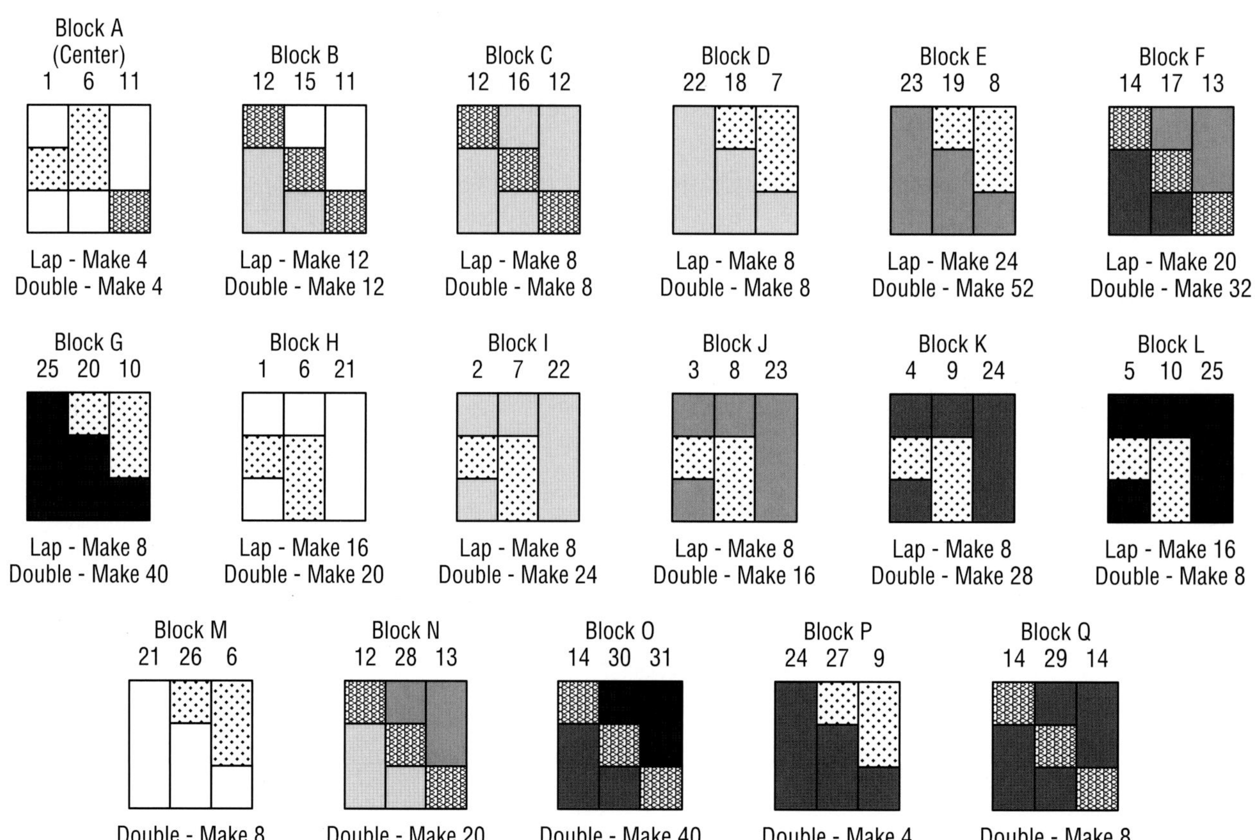

Plain Blocks

Blocks cut from 4¼"-wide strips are used between the pieced blocks to complete the design. Crosscut 4¼"-wide strips of fabric into 4¼" x 4¼" squares, following the chart below. Also use remaining 4¼"-wide strips.

		Number of Strips and Squares			
		Lap		*Dbl/Q*	
		Strips	Squares	Strips	Squares
Lightest	Z 1	1	8	1+	12
	Z 2	2+	20	5+	48
	Z 3	2+	24	6	52
	Z 4	3+	28	13	132
Darkest	Z 5	1	4	4	40

+ Indicates use of remaining 4¼"-wide strips

Quilt Top Assembly and Finishing

1. Arrange the blocks, following the quilt plan for the size you are making(page 60 or 61). Letters in the upper left fourth of the chart indicate placement of the pieced blocks. Be sure to place pieced blocks with the fabrics and seams oriented in the same direction as shown in the quilt plan.
2. Sew the blocks together, using the "pairs of pairs of pairs" assembly method described on page 16 in the General Directions.
3. Quilt, using your favorite method. Outline the hearts and then quilt diagonally through the lattice and rows of background.
4. Bind the edges of the quilt.

Marilla's Fireworks

by Jane St. Pierre

Jane St. Pierre, husband Walt, and their family moved to Durango in 1986 to enjoy the outdoors, and they chose a home in a native area outside of town. The mother of four sons, Devon, Brian, Preston, and Dwayne, Jane is now enjoying her two grandchildren, both girls. In her leisure time, she enjoys skiing and tennis.

When the setting sun dances and reflects off the neighboring mountains, it creates "alpenglow." Jane captured the light dancing off the snow of her beloved mountains in "Marilla's Fireworks."

Purgatory Ski Resort, located twenty-five miles north of Durango, offers runs for everyone, with slopes ranging from bunny to double diamond. When skiers take a day off from the slopes, they often come to Animas Quilts.

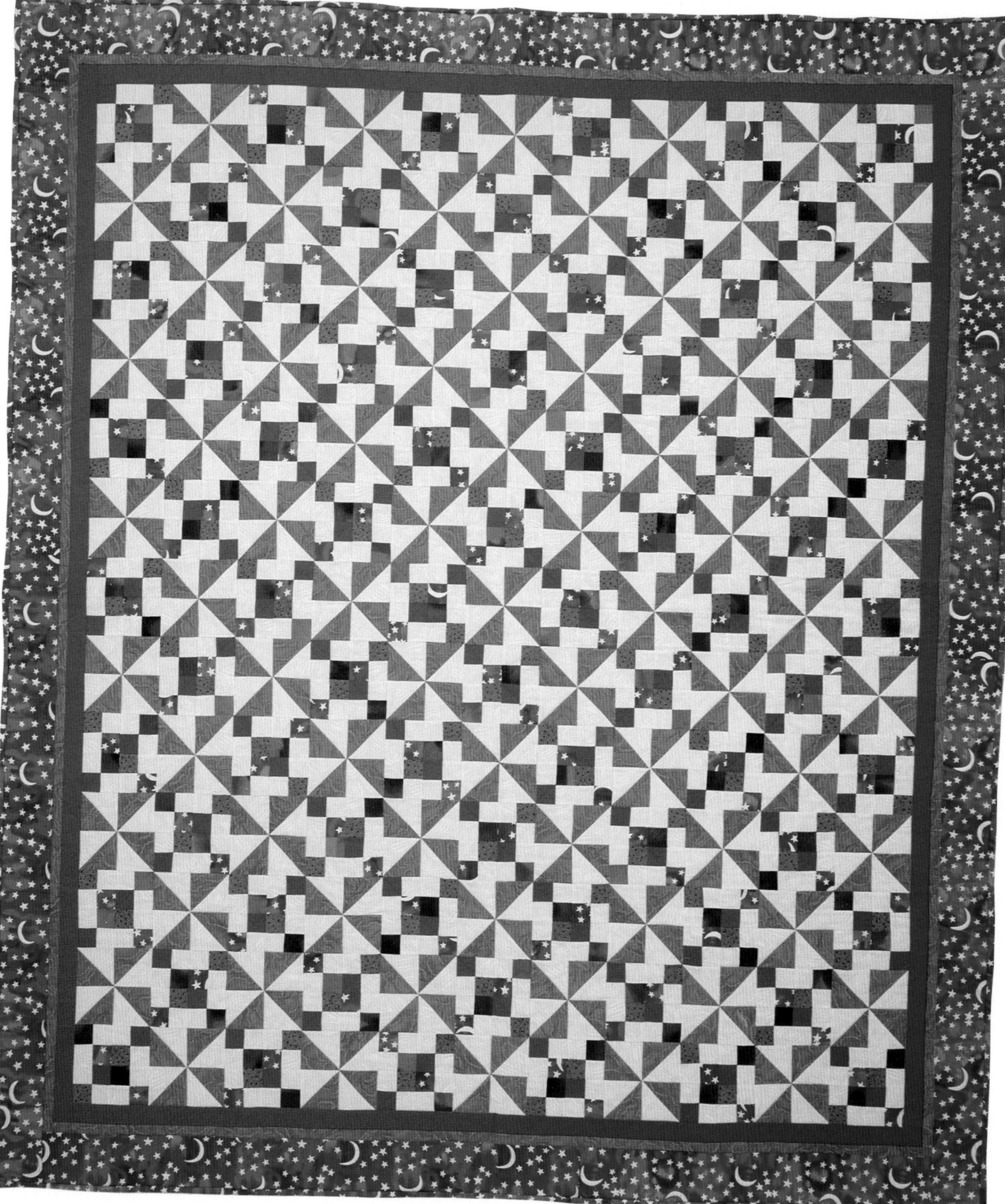

Marilla's Fireworks, by Jane St. Pierre, 1992, Durango, Colorado, 79" x 91".

Beginner

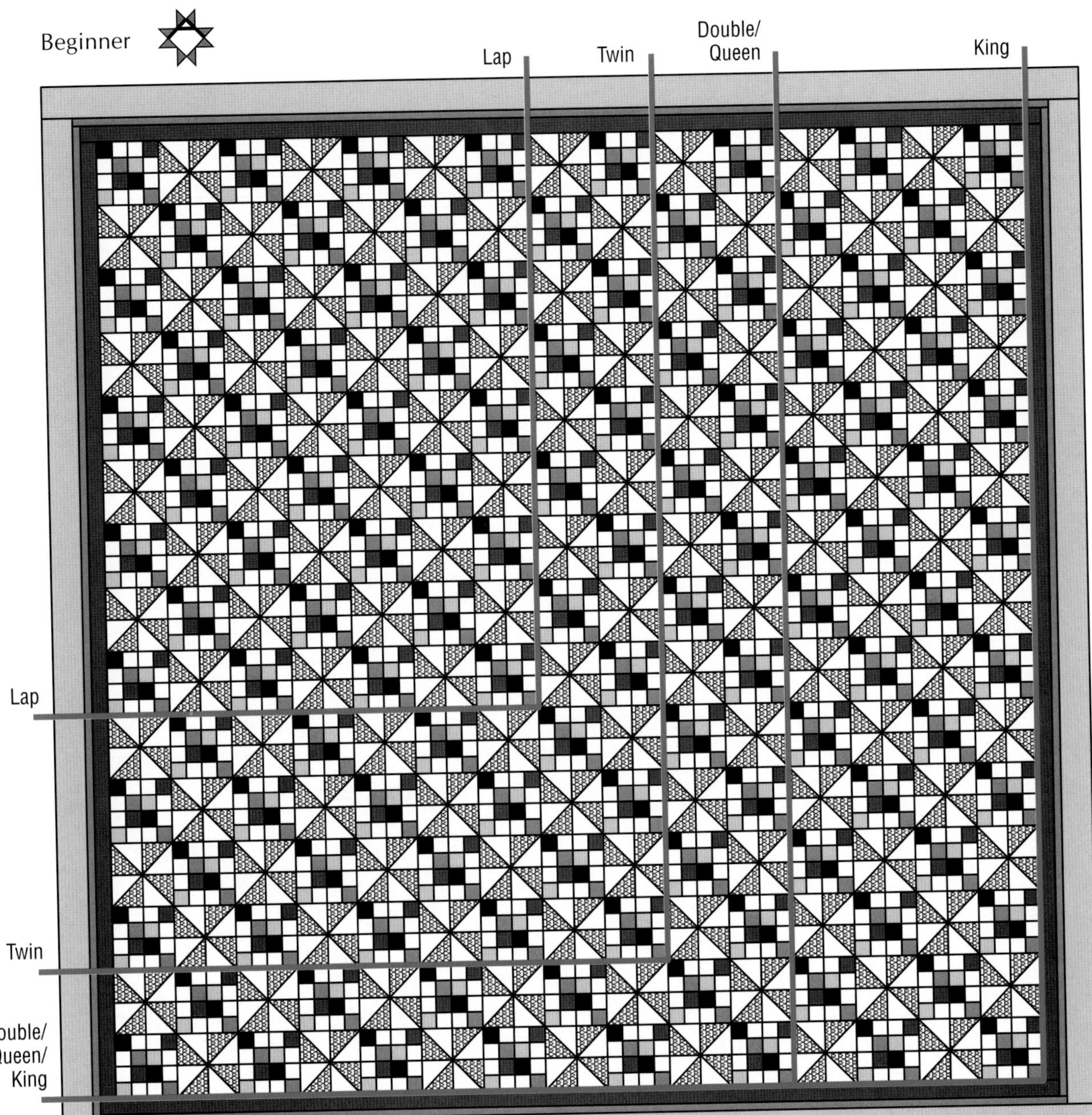

Quilt Plan

QUILT SIZES

Lap	*Twin*	*Dbl/Q*	*King*
Finished Size	**Finished Size**	**Finished Size**	**Finished Size**
55" x 67"	67" x 91"	79" x 103"	103" x 103"
No. of Blocks	**No. of Blocks**	**No. of Blocks**	**No. of Blocks**
63	117	165	225
Block Layout	**Block Layout**	**Block Layout**	**Block Layout**
7 x 9	9 x 13	11 x 15	15 x 15

Number of Blocks

	Crib/Lap	Twin	Dbl/Q	King
Block A	32	59	83	113
Block B	31	58	82	112

Block Size: 6"

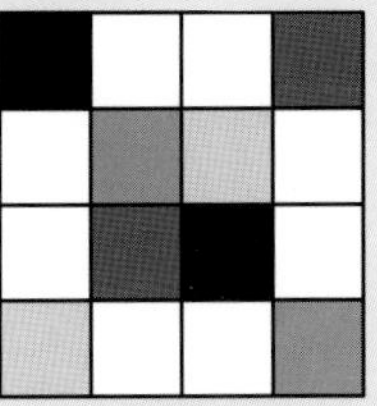
Block A

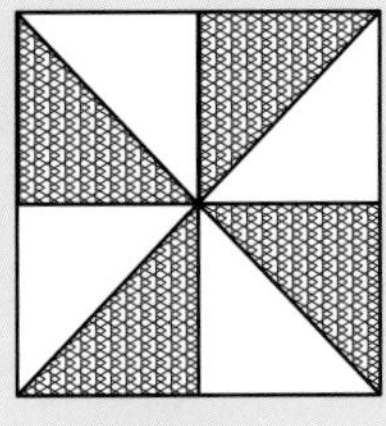
Block B

MATERIALS: 44"-wide fabric

Purchase the required yardage for the quilt size you are making.

Fabric Requirements in Yards

	Crib/Lap	*Twin*	*Dbl/Q*	*King*
4 Asst. Blues (Block A)*	1/4 each	3/8 each	1/2 each	2/3 each
Pink (Block B)	1	1 3/4	2 3/8	3
Background	1 1/2	3 1/4	4 3/4	5 3/4
Inner Border	1/3	3/8	1/2	5/8
Middle Border	1/4	1/3	3/8	1/2
Outer Border	7/8	1 1/8	1 1/4	1 3/8
Binding	2/3	3/4	1	1 1/3
Backing	3 3/8	5 1/2	6 1/8	9 1/4
Piecing for Backing	⊟	◫	◫	▥

*Select 4 different blues of similar value.

Cutting

Cut all strips across the width of the fabric (crosswise grain).

Block A

Assign each of the 4 blues a letter: W, X, Y, and Z. Always sew each of these to a background strip. See the chart at the top of page 70 for cutting the number of strips required for the quilt size you are making.

		Number of Strips			
Fabric	*Strip Width*	*Crib/Lap*	*Twin*	*Dbl/Q*	*King*
W	2"	4	6	8	11
X	2"	4	6	8	11
Y	2"	4	6	8	11
Z	2"	4	6	8	11
Background	2"	16	24	32	44

Directions

Block A

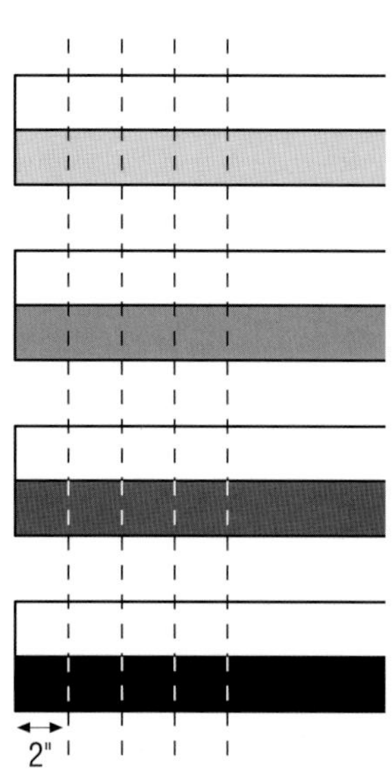

1. Sew each of the blue strips (W, X, Y, Z) to a background strip, using a ¼"-wide seam allowance. Press seams toward the darker fabric. Crosscut the strips into 2"-wide segments. See chart below.

	Number of Segments			
	Crib/Lap	*Twin*	*Dbl/Q*	*King*
W	64	118	166	226
X	64	118	166	226
Y	64	118	166	226
Z	64	118	166	226
Total 2" segments	256	472	664	904

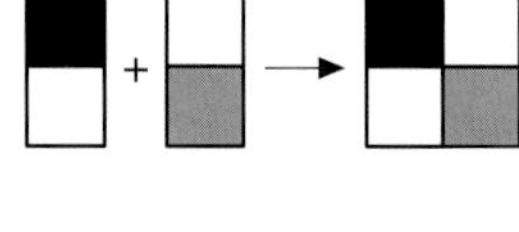

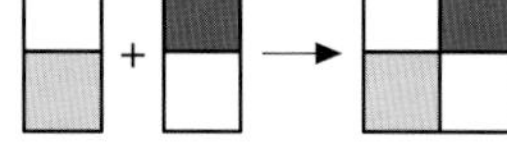

Make two kinds of Four Patches.

2. Sew the 2" segments into 2 different Four Patch blocks as shown at left. Create a scrappy look by sewing the same two-patch pieces together to form two different Four Patch blocks.

3. Assemble the different Four Patch blocks as shown below. Make the required number of Block A as shown in the chart on page 69.

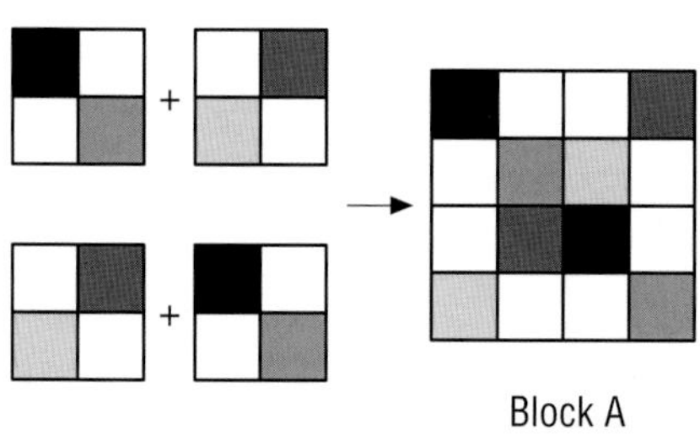

Block A

Block B

1. This block is made up of four half-square triangle units. The easiest way to make them is with a 3⅞" grid. Refer to the General Directions on pages 12–15 for specific instructions and see chart below for the number required.

	Number of Units			
	Crib/Lap	*Twin*	*Dbl/Q*	*King*
Half-Square Triangle Units	124	232	328	448

2. Sew half-square triangle units together to make a pinwheel as shown at right. Be consistent in the direction you "spin" the pinwheel. Make the required number of Block B as shown on page 69.

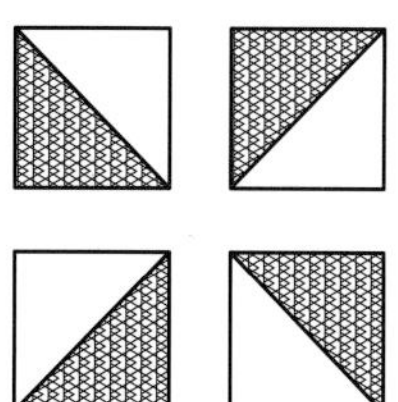

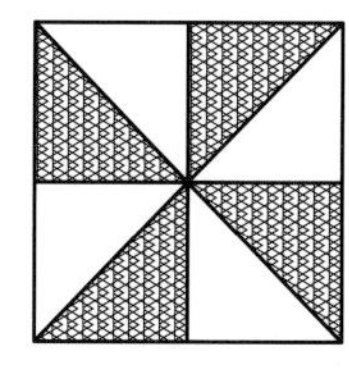

Block B

Quilt Top Assembly and Finishing

1. Arrange the blocks, alternating Block A and Block B, as shown in the quilt plan on page 68. Sew the blocks together, using the "pairs of pairs of pairs" assembly method described on page 12 in the General Directions. Press carefully.
2. Cut the required number of strips for each border and the binding, in the widths indicated in the chart below.

		Number of Strips			
Fabric	*Strip Width*	*Crib/Lap*	*Twin*	*Dbl/Q*	*King*
Inner Border	2"	5	6	8	9
Middle Border	1½"	5	7	8	9
Outer Border	4½"	6	8	9	10
Binding	3"	6	8	9	10

3. Sew the inner border strips together, end to end, and press seams open. Measure the quilt top for borders as shown on page 17. Sew inner borders to the sides of the quilt top, then to the top and bottom edges. Repeat for the middle and outer borders.
4. Quilt in diagonal rows through the center of each block and in-the-ditch around the pinwheels.
5. Bind the edges of the quilt.

Quilting Diagrams

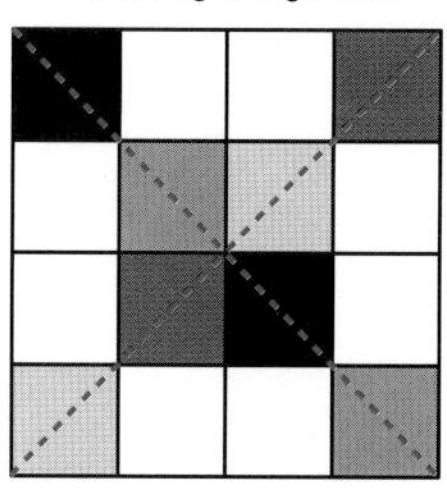

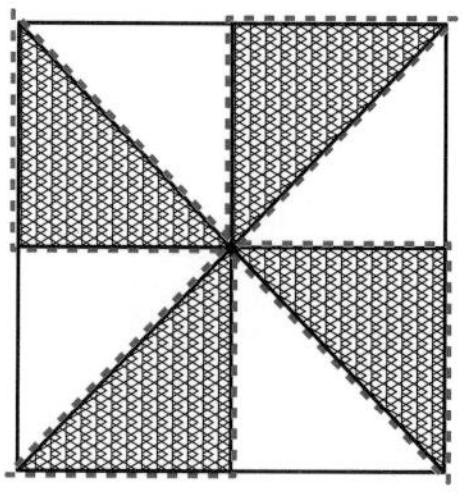

Las Parroquias

by Laura Bales

Laura Bales' quilt designing came naturally after artistic experiences in pottery, weaving, and macramé. She has an innate sense of design and sends it singing through her quilts. She and her husband, Bill, settled in Durango in 1987 after simply driving through this area and knowing they had found home. They enjoy their "blended" family of six children, Greg, Kelly, David, Stacey, Beth, and Scott. A gourmet cook, Laura also enjoys skiing, traveling, and hiking these hills with her two dogs.

Las Parroquias is Spanish for "The Steeples," and you can see the steeples in this design. Inspired by the Southwest influences around her, Laura designed this Native American-styled quilt.

She wanted her students to explore free-motion quilting so this quilt has large, open spaces. You too can discover how easy and fun it is to machine quilt!

The sun bathes Cliff Palace, the largest of Mesa Verde's cliff dwellings, built over seven hundred years ago. This structure has 217 rooms stacked in tiers up to four stories high and includes twenty-three kivas used by the clans of this Anasazi community.

Las Parroquias, by Laura Bales, 1992, Durango, Colorado, 49" x 76".

Advanced Beginner 

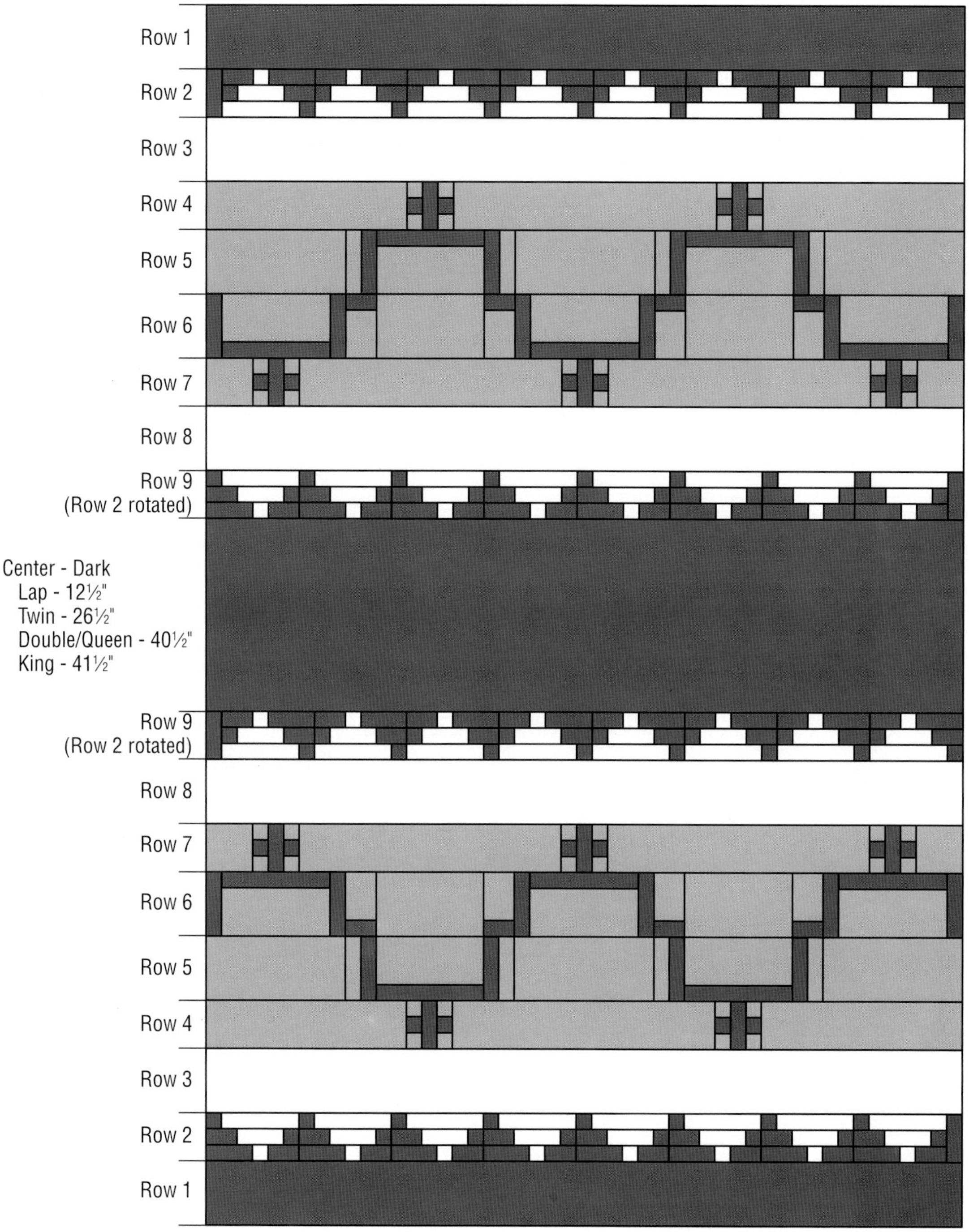

Row 1
Row 2
Row 3
Row 4
Row 5
Row 6
Row 7
Row 8
Row 9
(Row 2 rotated)

Center - Dark
Lap - 12½"
Twin - 26½"
Double/Queen - 40½"
King - 41½"

Row 9
(Row 2 rotated)
Row 8
Row 7
Row 6
Row 5
Row 4
Row 3
Row 2
Row 1

Quilt Plan

QUILT SIZES

Crib/Lap	*Twin*	*Dbl/Q*	*King*
Finished Size	**Finished Size**	**Finished Size**	**Finished Size**
49" x 76"	67" x 90"	85" x 104"	109" x 105"

MATERIALS: 44"-wide fabric

Purchase the required yardage for the quilt size you are making.

Fabric Requirements in Yards

	Crib/Lap	*Twin*	*Dbl/Q*	*King*
Medium-Light	1⅓	1⅔	2	2½
Medium	1½	1⅞	2⅓	2¾
Dark	2	3¼	4⅝	6
Binding	⅔	¾	1	1⅛
Backing	3⅛	5⅜	7⅔	9⅜
Piecing for Backing				

CUTTING

Cut all strips across the width of the fabric (crosswise grain).

		Number of Strips			
Fabric	*Strip Width*	*Crib/Lap*	*Twin*	*Dbl/Q*	*King*
Medium-Light	5½"	2	2	2	3
	4½"	5	7	9	11
	3½"	2	2	2	3
	1½"	2	2	2	3
Medium	4½"	3	4	5	5
	3½"	8	10	13	16
	1½"	3	4	5	7
Dark	4½"	3	4	5	7
	3½"	2	3	3	4
	2½"	3	4	4	6
	1½"	8	11	13	17
Binding	3"	7	8	10	11

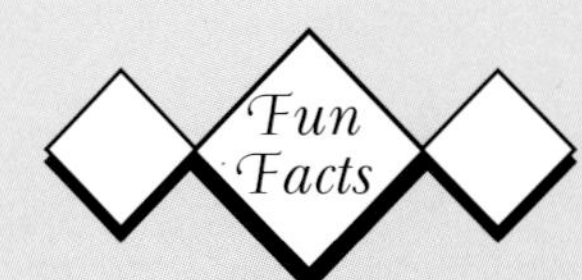

Parroquias is pronounced
Par-ro-key-as
(rolling the r's if you can).

Directions

This quilt is constructed by making two identical pieced "halves," which are joined with a center section of dark fabric. Each "half" is made up of nine rows. The instructions are organized by rows, with the pieced rows explained first.

Rows 2 and 9

1. Make the strip sets shown in the diagram at right. Press the seams toward the dark fabric; then crosscut the strip sets into 1½"-wide segments. Refer to the chart at the top of page 76 for the number of strips sets, segments, units, and the units per row required for the size quilt you are making.

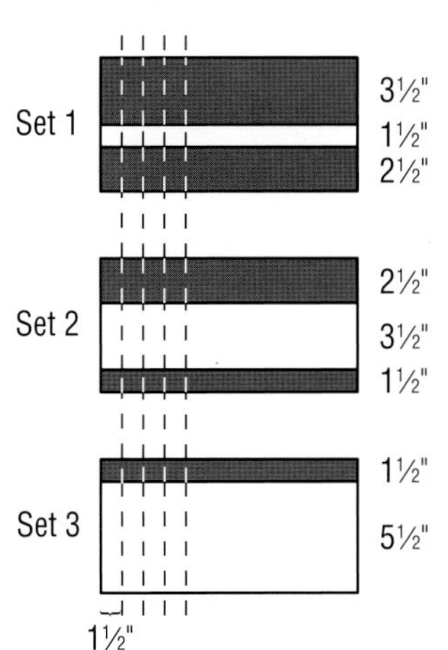

Number of Strip Sets and Segments

	Crib/Lap		Twin		Dbl/Q		King	
	Strip Sets	**1½" Segments**	**Strip Sets**	**1½" Segments**	**Strip Sets**	**1½" Segments**	**Strip Sets**	**1½" Segments**
Strip Set 1	1½*	32	2	44	2	56	3	72
Strip Set 2	1½*	32	2	44	2	56	3	72
Strip Set 3	1½*	32	2	44	2	56	3	72
*½ strip set is 21" long.								
Assembled Units	32		44		56		72	
Units Per Row	8		11		14		18	

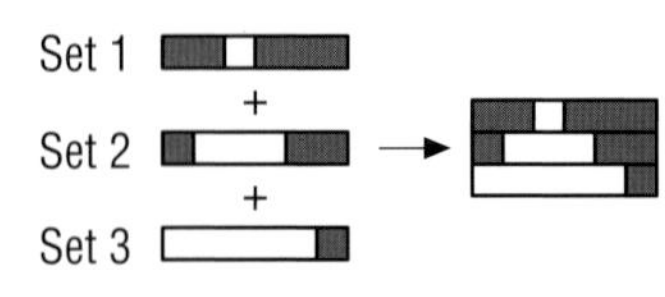

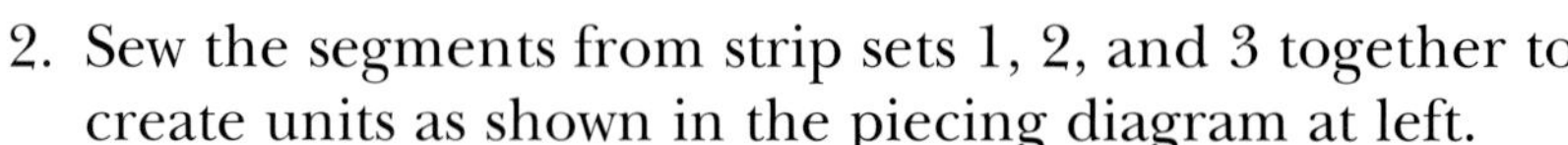

2. Sew the segments from strip sets 1, 2, and 3 together to create units as shown in the piecing diagram at left.

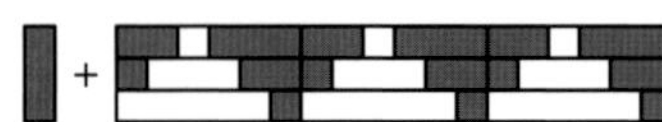

3. Sew the pieced units together to make 4 identical rows, 2 of row 2 and 2 of row 9. Refer to the chart above for the required number of units per row. Cut 4 rectangles, each 1½" x 3½", from a 3½"-wide strip of dark fabric; sew the rectangles to the left edge of each row.

Rows 4 and 7

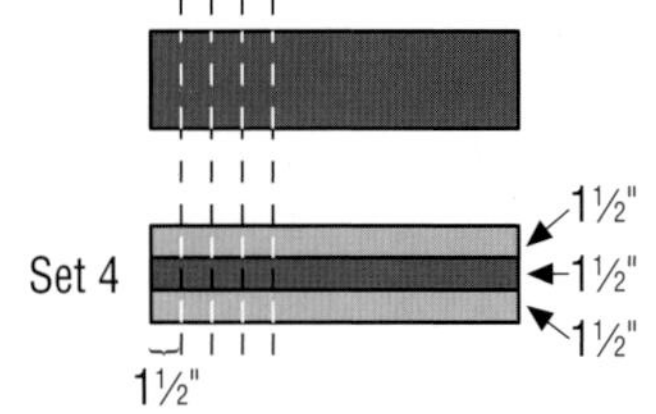

1. Make the strip sets as shown in the diagram at left. Press the seams toward the dark fabrics; then crosscut the assembled strip sets and a 3½"-wide dark strip into 1½"-wide segments. Refer to the chart below for the number of strip sets, segments, and units required.

Number of Strip Sets and Segments

	Crib/Lap		Twin		Dbl/Q		King	
	Strip Sets	**1½" Segments**	**Strip Sets**	**1½" Segments**	**Strip Sets**	**1½" Segments**	**Strip Sets**	**1½" Segments**
Strip Set 4	1	20	1	28	1½*	36	2	44
Dark Strip-3½"	½*	10	1	14	1	18	1	22
*½ strip set is 21" long.								
Assembled Units	10		14		18		22	

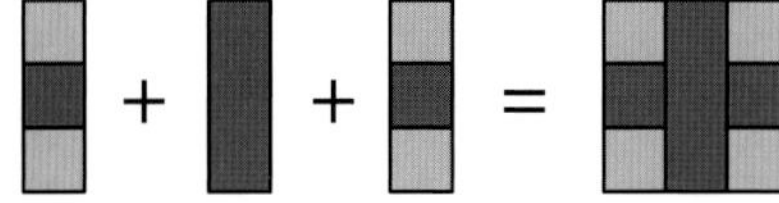

2. Sew the segments from strip set 4 and from the dark strip together to create Ninepatch units as shown at left.

3. For row 4, crosscut 3½"-wide medium strips into the segments for the quilt size you are making, following the chart at right.

	Segments	Size
Crib/Lap	4	13½" x 3½"
	2	17½" x 3½"
Twin	4	2½" x 3½"
	6	17½" x 3½"
Dbl/Q	4	11½" x 3½"
	6	17½" x 3½"
King	4	3½" x 3½"
	10	17½" x 3½"

4. Sew the Ninepatch units and 3½"-wide segments of medium fabric into rows as shown below. Make 2 of row 4.

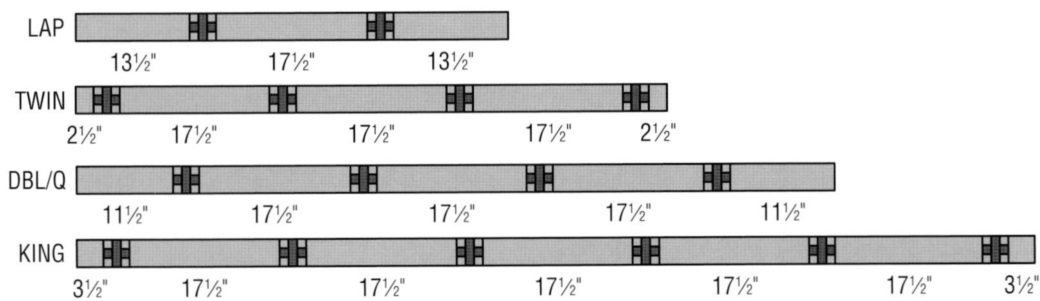

5. For row 7, crosscut 3½"-wide medium strips into segments, following the chart at right.

	Segments	Size
Crib/Lap	4	3½" x 3½"
	4	17½" x 3½"
Twin	4	12½" x 3½"
	4	17½" x 3½"
Dbl/Q	4	1½" x 3½"
	8	17½" x 3½"
King	4	13½" x 3½"
	8	17½" x 3½"

6. Sew the Ninepatch units and 3½"-wide segments of medium fabric into rows as shown below. Make 2 of row 7.

LAP
3½" 17½" 17½" 3½"
TWIN
12½" 17½" 17½" 12½"
DBL/Q
1½" 17½" 17½" 17½" 17½" 1½"
KING
13½" 17½" 17½" 17½" 17½" 13½"

Row 5

1. Make strip sets as shown in the diagram at right. Press the seams toward the dark fabric; then crosscut the strip sets into segments, following the chart at the top of page 78. Crosscut 4½"-wide strips of medium and dark fabrics, as indicated in the chart.

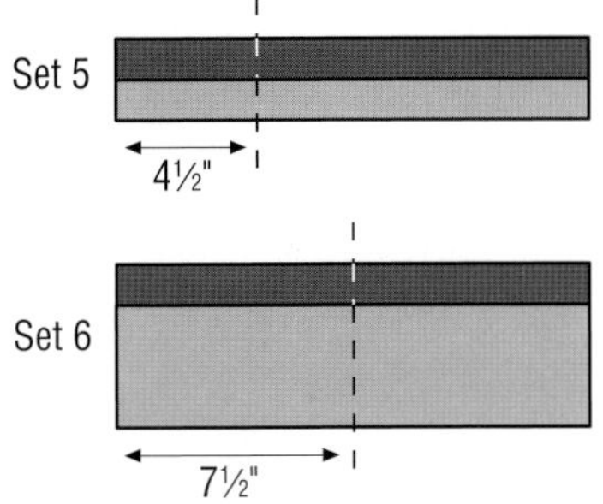

Note: Strip set 6 is also used in row 6. The number of strip sets includes enough for row 6; however, directions for crosscutting the row 6 strip set are included in that section.

	Crib/Lap			Twin			Dbl/Q			King		
	Strip Sets	Segments	Segment Width	Strip Sets	Segments	Segment Width	Strip Sets	Segments	Segment Width	Strip Sets	Segments	Segment Width
Strip Set 5	1	8	4½"	1½*	12	4½"	2	16	4½"	2½*	20	4½"
Strip Set 6	2½*	4	7½"	4	8	7½"	5	8	7½"	6	12	7½"
Med. Strip	2	6	9½"	2	6	9½"	3	4	7½"	2½*	10	9½"
								6	9½"			
Dark Strip										½*	4	1½"

*½ strip set is 21" long.

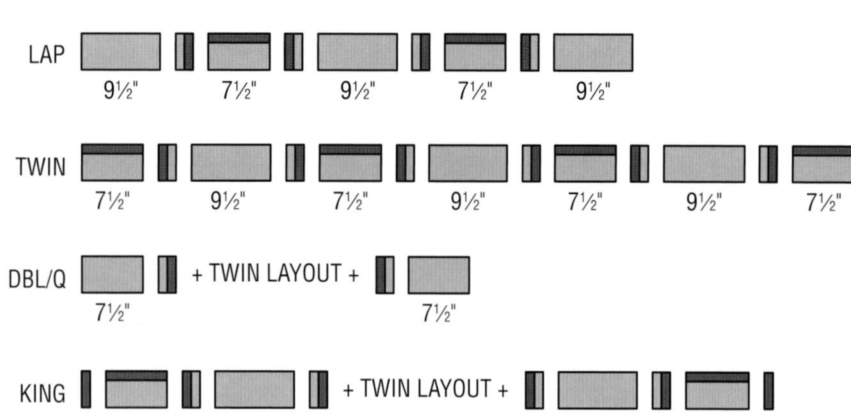

2. Sew the segments from strip sets 5 and 6 and from the medium and dark strips together as shown at left. Make 2 rows. You will not use all of strip set 6. Set remainder aside for step 1 of row 6.

Row 6

1. Using the remainder of strip set 6, crosscut the strip sets into segments as shown in the chart below.

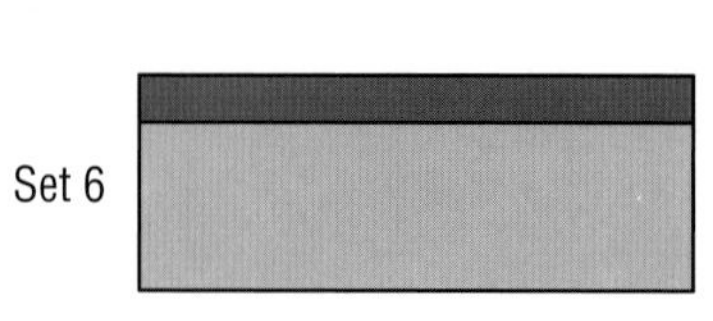

		Number of Segments			
	Segment Width	Crib/Lap	Twin	Dbl/Q	King
Strip Set 6	1½"				4
	2½"	8	12	16	20
	6½"			4	
	7½"	6	6	6	10

2. Crosscut 4½"-wide strips of medium and dark fabric into segments as shown in the chart below.

Number of Strips and Segments

	Segment Width	Crib/Lap		Twin		Dbl/Q		King	
		Strips	Segments	Strips	Segments	Strips	Segments	Strips	Segments
Med.	7½"	1	4	2	8	2	8	2½*	12
Dark	1½"	½*	12	½*	12	1	16	1	20

*½ strip is 21" long.

3. Sew the segments from strip set 6 and from the medium and dark strips together as shown at right. Make 2 rows.

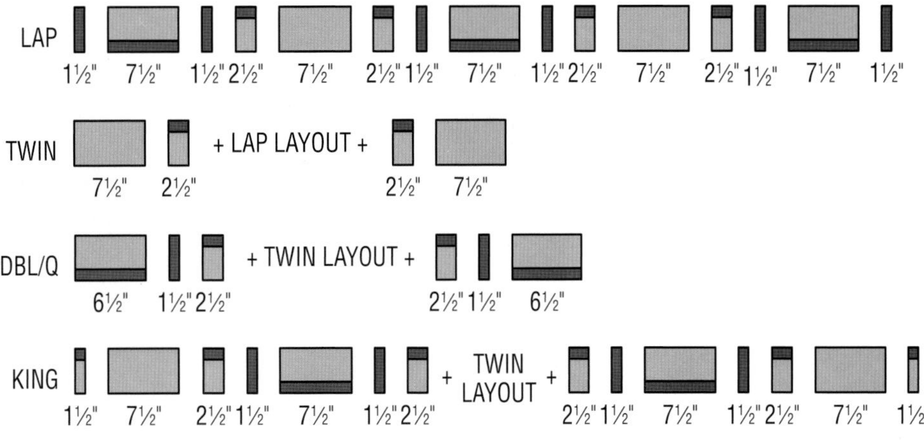

Rows 1, 3, and 8

These rows are a snap! Use 4½"-wide strips of dark fabric for row 1. Use 4½"-wide strips of medium-light fabric for rows 3 and 8.

Sew strips of fabric for each row, end to end, with ¼"-wide seams and press seams open. Cut to the required length (the width of the quilt) as shown below.

Note: The following measurements are based on perfect ¼"-wide seams in all your sewing. Measure the length of your finished sections to find your "actual" length and cut to that length if different from measurement given below.

	Crib/Lap	*Twin*	*Dbl/Q*	*King*
Row 1 (4½"-wide dark)	49½"	67½"	85½"	109½"
Row 3 (4½"-wide med.-light.)	49½"	67½"	85½"	109½"
Row 8 (4½"-wide med.-light.)	49½"	67½"	85½"	109½"

Quilt Top Assembly and Finishing

1. Sew rows 1–9 together, following the quilt plan on page 74. Be aware that while rows 2 and 9 are identical, row 9 is turned upside down. Make 2 identical halves.
2. Cut the center section from dark fabric. See chart at right.
3. Now, connect the 2 halves with a section of dark fabric in the center. Be sure to orient each half as shown in the quilt plan on page 74.
4. Quilt as desired. To quilt it as Laura did, outline quilt first. Then, using free-motion machine quilting, echo quilt rows 2 and 9. Using the bear template (page 87), trace bears in the center section (Lap—3 bears, Twin—4 bears, Dbl/Q—5 bears, King—6 bears) and quilt on the traced lines. Finally, stipple quilt in all the open areas.
5. Bind the edges of the quilt.

Cutting for center section:

* Lap: Cut 2 pieces, each 12½" wide, across the width of the fabric. Sew pieces together at the short ends and trim to 49½".
* Twin: Cut 2 pieces, each 26½" wide, across the width of the fabric. Sew pieces together at the short ends and trim to 67½".
* Dbl/Q: From the length of the fabric, cut 1 piece 40½" x 85½".
* King: From the length of the fabric, cut 1 piece 41½" x 109½".

Sky Tracks

by Debbie Houser

Debbie Houser has been in Colorado only a few years. She and Richard and their three daughters, Leticia, Ashley, and Kelsey, lived in Ouray, sometimes called the Switzerland of Colorado, before moving to Durango. An avid antique collector, Debbie is also an outdoor enthusiast. We enjoy the time she spends with us at Animas Quilts.

Debbie says, "There are many diverse distractions that seize our attention and lead us off into unknown territory—a shape, a color, a star in the night sky, a track pushed into the soft earth. This is the theme of 'Sky Tracks' as it captures the pearl-like gleam of the Colorado sky in its background. The bright yellow smile of the sun is in its star, and they are connected through bear tracks in the clouds of the sky."

The color of autumn in this corner of the mountains is gold—leaves shimmering on the trees like nuggets in stream beds. Aspens are affectionately called "Quakies" because of the sound made by their leaves when the breeze rushes through them.

Sky Tracks, by Debbie Houser, 1993, Durango, Colorado, 75" x 90".

Beginner

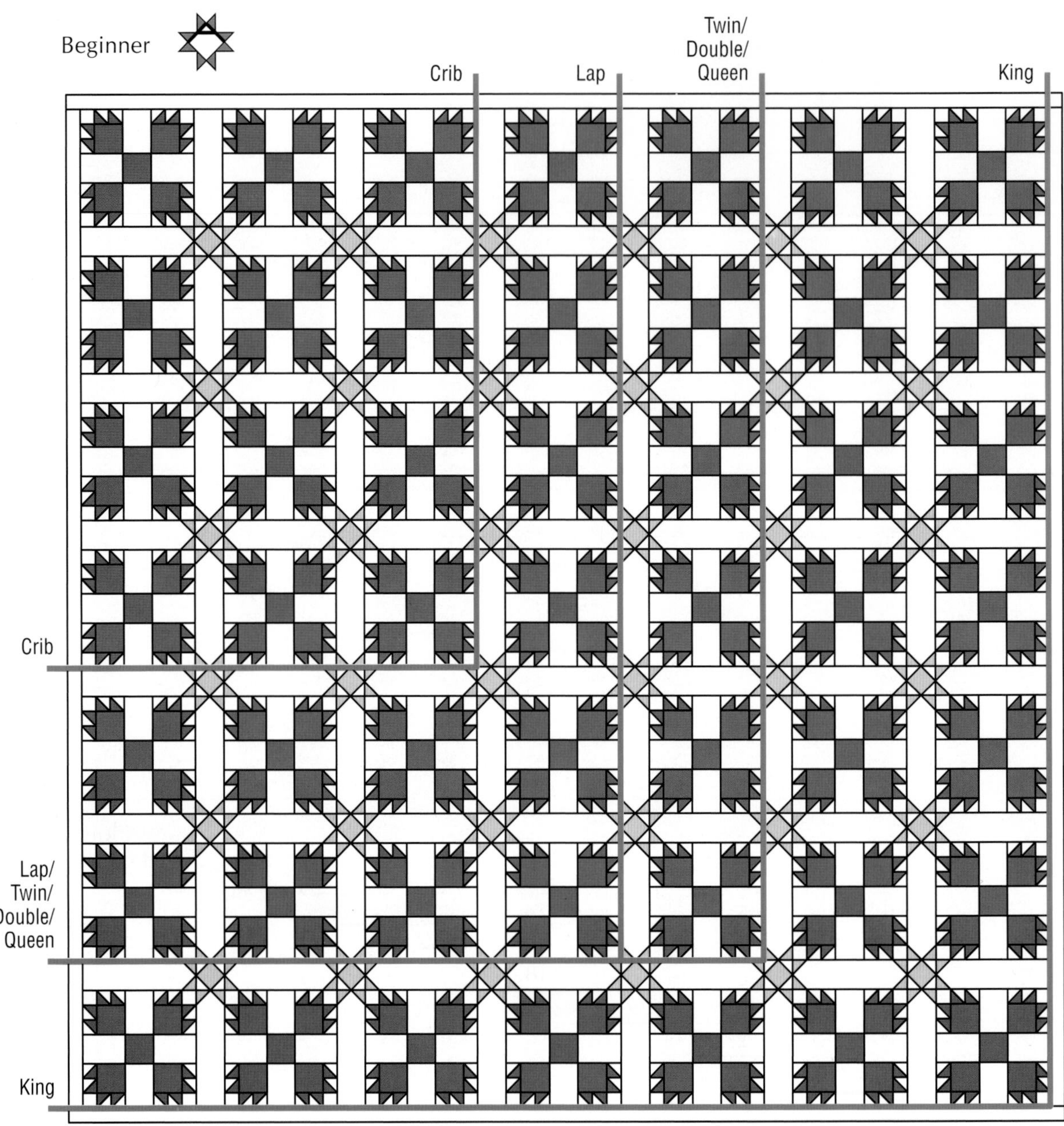

Quilt Plan

QUILT SIZES

Crib	*Lap*	*Twin**	*Dbl/Q**	*King*
Finished Size 45" x 60"	**Finished Size** 60" x 90"	**Finished Size** 75" x 90"	**Finished Size** 80" x 95"	**Finished Size** 105" x 105"
No. of Blocks 12	**No. of Blocks** 24	**No. of Blocks** 30	**No. of Blocks** 30	**No. of Blocks** 49
Block Layout 3 x 4	**Block Layout** 4 x 6	**Block Layout** 5 x 6	**Block Layout** 5 x 6	**Block Layout** 7 x 7

**The only difference between the Twin and Dbl/Q sizes is the width of the border. They both contain the same number of blocks and are assembled in the same manner.*

MATERIALS: 44"-wide fabric

Purchase the required yardage for the quilt size you are making.

Fabric Requirements in Yards

	Crib	*Lap*	*Twin*	*Dbl/Q*	*King*
Bear's Paw	1 1/8	2	2 5/8	2 5/8	4 1/4
Star	1/3	5/8	3/4	3/4	1 3/8
Background	2 1/2	4 1/2	5 2/3	6 1/3	9 1/4
Binding	5/8	3/4	7/8	7/8	1
Backing	2 7/8	5 3/8	5 3/8	5 2/3	9 3/8
Piecing for Backing					

Block Size: 12"

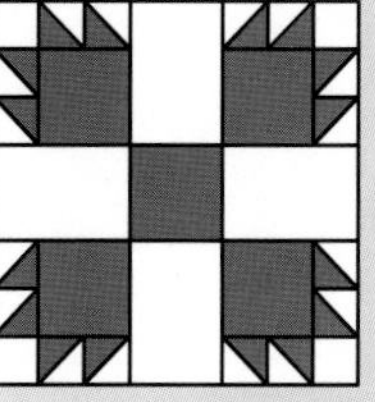

Bear's Paw Block

CUTTING

Cut all strips across the width of the fabric (crosswise grain).

CRIB QUILT

	First Cut		Second Cut	
Fabric	**Strips**	**Strip Width**	**Segments**	**Dimensions**
		Bear's Paw Blocks		
Background	3	2"	48	2" x 2"
	6	3 1/2"	48	3 1/2" x 5"
Bear's Paw	5	3 1/2"	60	3 1/2" x 3 1/2"
		Sashing		
Background	6	3 1/2"	17	3 1/2" x 12 1/2"
Star	3	2"	48	2" x 2"
		Cornerstones		
Background	2	2"	24	2" x 2"
Star	1	3 1/2"	6	3 1/2" x 3 1/2"

LAP QUILT

	First Cut		Second Cut	
Fabric	**Strips**	**Strip Width**	**Segments**	**Dimensions**
		Bear's Paw Blocks		
Background	5	2"	96	2" x 2"
	12	3 1/2"	96	3 1/2" x 5"
Bear's Paw	10	3 1/2"	120	3 1/2" x 3 1/2"
		Sashing		
Background	13	3 1/2"	38	3 1/2" x 12 1/2"
Star	6	2"	120	2" x 2"
		Cornerstones		
Background	3	2"	60	2" x 2"
Star	2	3 1/2"	15	3 1/2" x 3 1/2"

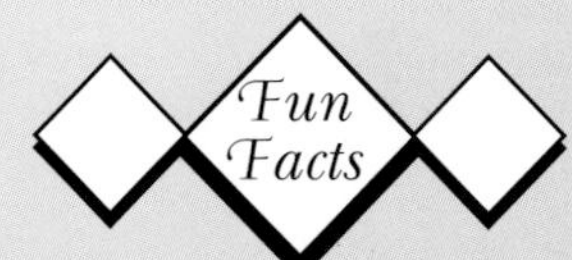

The late Louis L'Amour wrote many of his books from a room just above the Diamond Belle Saloon in the Strater Hotel. He liked the sound of the ragtime piano to place him in the proper mood.

TWIN/DBL/Q QUILT				
	First Cut		Second Cut	
Fabric	Strips	Strip Width	Segments	Dimensions
Bear's Paw Blocks				
Background	6	2"	120	2" x 2"
	15	3½"	120	3½" x 5"
Bear's Paw	13	3½"	150	3½" x 3½"
Sashing				
Background	17	3½"	49	3½" x 12½"
Star	8	2"	160	2" x 2"
Cornerstones				
Background	4	2"	80	2" x 2"
Star	2	3½"	20	3½" x 3½"

KING QUILT				
	First Cut		Second Cut	
Fabric	Strips	Strip Width	Segments	Dimensions
Bear's Paw Blocks				
Background	10	2"	196	2" x 2"
	25	3½"	196	3½" x 5"
Bear's Paw	21	3½"	245	3½" x 3½"
Sashing				
Background	28	3½"	84	3½" x 12½"
Star	15	2"	288	2" x 2"
Cornerstones				
Background	8	2"	144	2" x 2"
Star	4	3½"	36	3½" x 3½"

Bear's Paw Blocks

1. Make half-square triangle units from Bear's Paw and background fabrics, using your favorite method (see pages 12–15). The finished size of the units is 1½" x 1½". If using the grid method, draw squares 2⅜" x 2⅜". See chart below for the number of squares you need to draw to make the number of half-square triangle units for the size you are making.

	Crib	*Lap*	*Twin/Dbl/Q*	*King*
No. of Squares	96	192	240	392
No. of Half-Square Triangle Units	192	384	480	784

2. Press seams toward the darker fabric.
3. Assemble Bear's Paw blocks as shown in the piecing diagram at the top of page 85. Make the required number of blocks. (See page 82.)

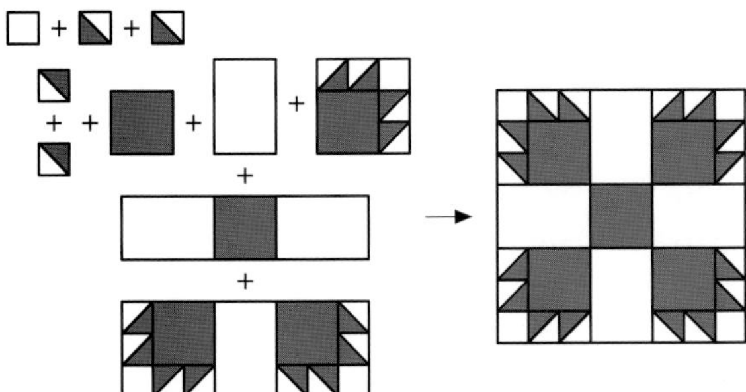

Sashing and Cornerstones

The sashing units are made with diagonal corners at the short ends. The diagonal corners combined with the pieced cornerstone create the stars between the Bear's Paw blocks. Some sashing units have diagonal corners at all four corners; some sashing units have only two diagonal corners at one end. Make the required number of sashing units and cornerstones, following the chart below.

	Number of Units			
	Crib	*Lap*	*Twin/Dbl/Q*	*King*
Sashing Units with 4 Diagonal Corners	7	22	31	60
Sashing Units with 2 Diagonal Corners	10	16	18	24
Cornerstones	6	15	20	36

Pieced Sashing

1. Place a 2" x 2" square of star fabric on one corner of a 3½" x 12½" sashing strip, right sides together. Stitch diagonally across the 2" square, from an outside corner to the opposite corner, as shown at right.
2. Trim the excess star fabric to ¼" from stitching line and press the star fabric toward the corner. Do not trim the corners of the background rectangle.
3. Repeat this process for the remaining 1 or 3 corners on each sashing strip. Make the required number of sashing units. (See chart above.)

4 diagonal corners

2 diagonal corners

Pieced Cornerstones

The cornerstones are joined with the sashing units to make the stars.

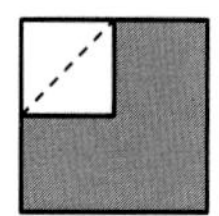
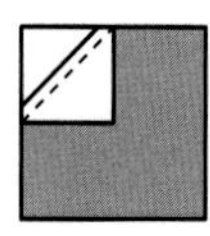
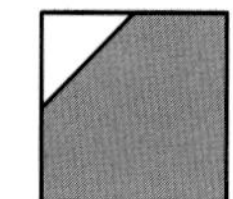

1. Place a 2" square of background fabric on one corner of the 3½" square of star fabric. Stitch diagonally across the 2" square, from an outside corner to the opposite corner, as shown at left. Trim the excess background square ¼" from stitching line and press the star fabric toward the corner.

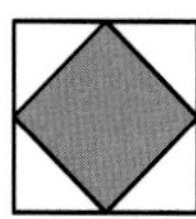

2. Repeat this process for the remaining 3 corners on each 3½" square. Make the required number of pieced cornerstones. (See chart on page 85.)

That's it! All the pieces are made and it's time to put your Sky Tracks quilt top together.

Quilt Top Assembly and Finishing

1. Arrange the Bear Paw's blocks, pieced sashing units, and pieced cornerstones as shown in the quilt plan on page 82. Be sure to orient the sashing strips as shown to create the star.
2. Sew the blocks together, using the "pairs of pairs of pairs" assembly method described on page 12 in the General Directions.
3. Cut 2"-wide border and binding strips as shown in the chart below.

Note: Cut 4½"-wide border strips for the Dbl/Q size only.

		Number of Strips			
Fabric	***Strip Width***	***Crib/Lap***	***Twin***	***Dbl/Q***	***King***
Border	2"	6	8		11
	4½"			9	
Binding	3"	6	8	9	11

4. Sew the border strips together, end to end, and press the seams open. Measure the quilt top for borders as shown on page 17. Sew the border to the sides of the quilt top, then to the top and bottom edges.
5. Quilt as desired, using your favorite method.
6. Bind the edges of the quilt.

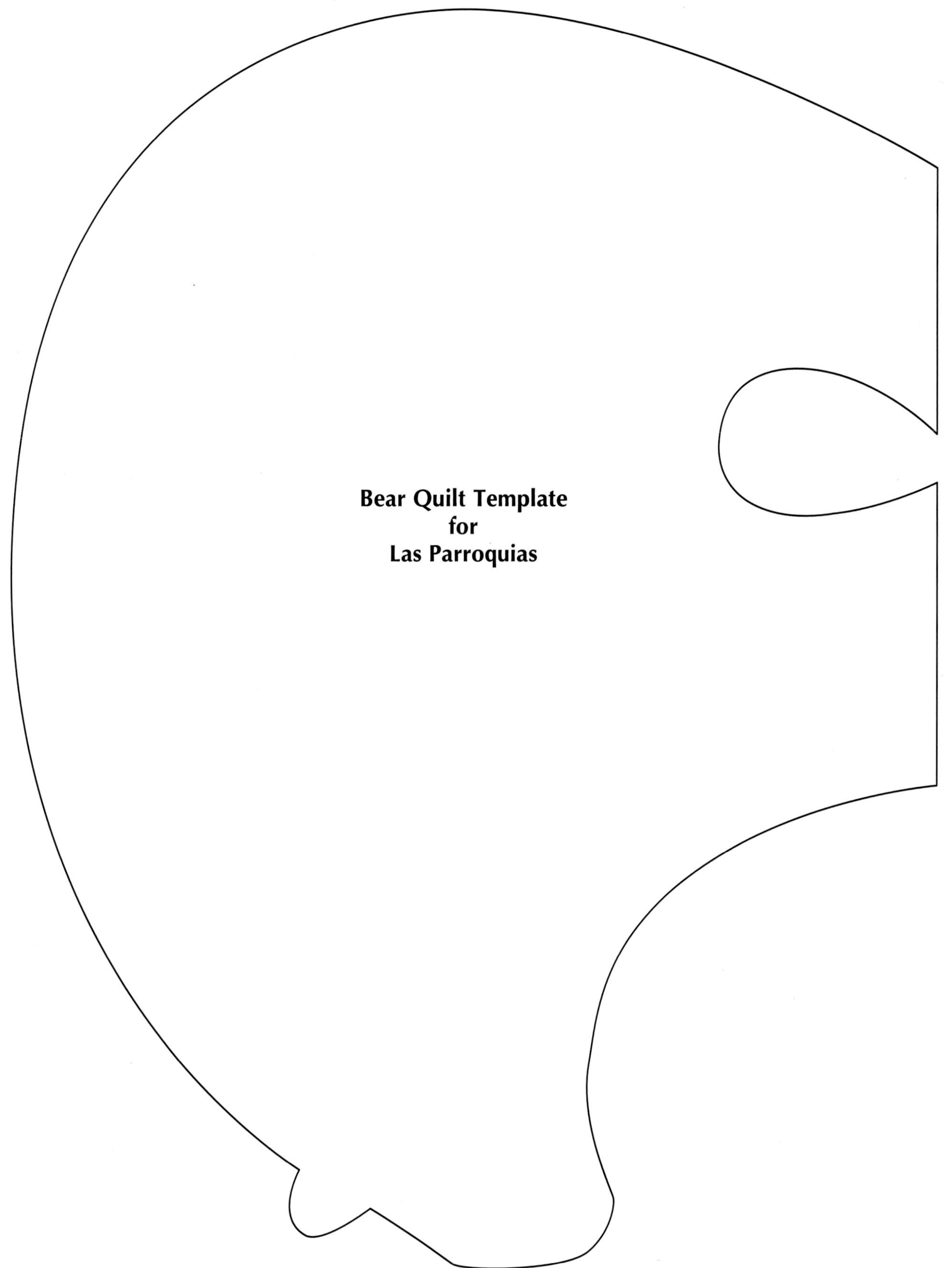
Bear Quilt Template
for
Las Parroquias

Product Information

Most of the products listed here are available at your favorite quilt shop. If, however, you are unable to find them, we do offer a mail-order service.

Additionally, Jackie's books are all available by mail: (Add $1 postage for one book and an extra 50¢ for each additional book.)

Chains of Love (Irish Chain variations) - $10

Star Gazing (Ohio Stars and variations) - $12

Perennial Patchwork (8 pieced flowers) - $11

Weaver Fever (bargello woven design) - $6.50

Quadcentrics (designs that twist) - $7

Tessellations (geometrics with an Escher-ish feeling) - $12

Dining Dazzle (placemats and table runners) - $16

Send order to: Animas Quilts
600 Main Avenue
Durango, CO 81301

We are importers of the gorgeous Bou BouDima fabric seen in Star of the Southwest. These fabrics come from Holland. For 4" x 4" swatches of the 30 most exciting Bou BouDima fabrics, send $10 to the above address.

The Binding Miter Tool, shown on page 21, will help you mark double miters for common angles. To order, send $4, plus $1 for postage and handling to the above address.